100 LANGUAGE GAMES

FOR AGES 3 TO 5

Easy-to-play games

Supporting early learning

Stages of development

JILLIAN HARKER

D0185426

CREDITS

British Library Cataloguing-in-Publication Data A catalogue record for this book is available from the British Library.

ISBN 0 439 98458 0

The right of Jillian Harker to be identified as the author of this work has been asserted by her in accordance with the Copyright, Designs and Patents Act 1988.

All rights reserved. This book is sold subject to the condition that it shall not, by way of trade or otherwise, be lent, hired out or otherwise circulated without the publisher's prior consent in any form of binding or cover other than that in which it is published and without a similar condition, including this condition, being imposed upon the subsequent purchaser.

No part of this publication may be reproduced, stored in a retrieval system, or transmitted, in any form or by any means, electronic, mechanical, photocopying, recording or otherwise, without the prior permission of the publisher. This book remains copyright, although permission is granted to copy pages where indicated for classroom distribution and use only in the school which has purchased the book, or by the teacher who has purchased the book, and in accordance with the CLA licensing agreement. Photocopying permission is given only for purchasers and not for borrowers of books from any lending service.

Author
Jillian Harker

Illustrations
Gaynor Berry

Editor
Lesley Sudlow

Assistant Editor
Victoria Lee

Series Designer
Anna Oliwa

Designer
Anna Oliwa

Text © 2003 Jillian Harker
© 2003 Scholastic Ltd

Designed using Adobe PageMaker

Published by Scholastic Ltd
Villiers House
Clarendon Avenue
Leamington Spa
Warwickshire CV32 5PR

Visit our website at www.scholastic.co.uk
Printed by Belmont Press

1 2 3 4 5 6 7 8 9 0   3 4 5 6 7 8 9 0 1 2

Acknowledgements

The publishers gratefully acknowledge permission to reproduce the following copyright material:

© **2003, Comstock, Inc:** p24

© **Corbis:** p10

© **Ingram Publishing:** Cover, p1, p3, p4

© **Photodisc:** p4

© **Clara Von Aich/SODA:** p52, p53

© **Stanley Bach/SODA:** p76

© **John Fortunato/SODA:** p6, p8, p9, p11, p16, p23, p25, p26, p38, p59, p65, p68, p74, p98, p99, p105, p107, p109, p113, p114, p119

© **Dan Howell/SODA:** p14, p21, p90, p95, p96, p101, p124

© **Richard Hutchins/SODA:** p83

© **Ken Karp/SODA:** p35, p39

© **James Levin/SODA:** p24, p28, p29, p33, p37, p47, p51, p54, p61, p70, p82, p85, p122

© **David Mager/SODA:** p52, p97, p100

© **Ana Esperanza Nance/SODA:** p5, p10, p41, p43

© **Dan Powell/SODA:** p58, p75, p111, p112

© **Francis Clark Westfield/SODA:** p7, p67, p69

© **Ross Whitaker/SODA:** p15, p63, p66, p84, p93, p98

© **Stockbyte:** Cover, p1, p3

Every effort has been made to trace copyright holders and the publishers apologise for any inadvertent omissions.

CONTENTS

CHAPTER 1

CHAPTER 2

CHAPTER 3

CHAPTER 4

CONTENTS

CHAPTER 5

CHAPTER 6

CHAPTER 7

CHAPTER 8

INTRODUCTION

The importance of language skills

Language is a unique tool. It gives us the power to express feelings, to think and to organise our thoughts, to acquire information, to plan for the future and to remember the past. Language is also the vehicle for all learning. A child who enters school with well-developed language skills has already embarked on a learning adventure that embraces many of the subjects that he will encounter during his school years. In mastering the vocabulary of number, size, position and comparison, he has taken his first steps into the world of mathematics. As he predicts the outcome of his experiments with sand and water, he is making forays into the world of science. When he talks about his favourite books and scribbles a note to his teddy, he is showing interest in the magic of the written word.

The young child's spoken language provides the foundation on which all future learning is laid down. You are providing him with the best possible basis for the learning that he will encounter in school, and throughout his life.

Child development stages

Between the ages of three and five, children make significant advances in their acquisition of language. They acquire the vocabulary of size and position, and learn the names of colours. They develop their ability to give a correct account of recent events and experiences, and to listen to, and tell, long stories. They move from being able to produce simple three-word sentences to a point where they can create complex sentences, using conjunctions, such as 'and' or 'but', and can understand sentences that contain a number of clauses.

It is during this phase that the distinction between fact and fiction becomes clear in their minds. They learn to understand the concept of time and to use more advanced verb tenses such as past and future. This is a key point in a child's intellectual and social growth. Once the concept of time is in place, children are able to use this to control personal behaviour. They learn, for example, to postpone gratification, understanding that they may not be able to have something that they want immediately.

By the age of five, children use language as a tool for reasoning and problem-solving. They develop the skill of asking meaningful questions. Earlier use of the question words 'what' and 'where' is expanded to include 'who' and, most particularly, 'why' and 'how'.

The introduction to each chapter in this book will provide you with detailed information about particular aspects of language learning, and offer suggestions as to how you can help your child to develop skills in these areas.

Early learning

An understanding of how young children learn is essential if we are to provide effective learning opportunities. Children learn best from experiences that are active and concrete. Looking, touching, moving and exploring are the young child's route to learning. Games make an effective learning tool, because they provide a combination of action and concreteness. Since young children are always ready to learn at their own level, it is essential to ensure that any learning activity is at the correct level for your child's stage of development. In this way, success is assured and the desire to learn more is strengthened.

It is also important to understand that different children learn in different ways. Some children learn best when they can be very physically active; others are helped by the stimulus of visual material, since they find it difficult to take in lots of spoken language.

Ideal activities for young children will provide a variety of approaches, part concrete or visual stimulus, part spoken information and part opportunity to be active. Such activities will allow for a variety of different learning styles. As you try out games with your child, you will become aware of his particular learning style and become adept at choosing activities that suit that style.

Finally, it helps if we bear in mind that children learn language through listening to those around them and experimenting with language themselves. It is undoubtedly true that a child who experiences a language-rich environment will have a head start in this learning process. A child who has the opportunity to converse, to question, to explore books and print of every sort, and who sees those around him enjoying spoken and written communication, will be well on the way to acquiring good language skills.

Foundation Stage

The Qualifications and Curriculum Authority (QCA) has published the *Curriculum Guidance for the Foundation Stage* to guide parents and early years practitioners in providing activities and experiences to help children to progress in their development and learning. The document is divided into six Areas of Learning. In each Area, there are Early Learning Goals that describe the levels expected to be achieved by the end of the Foundation Stage. There are also Stepping Stones relating to knowledge and skills that adults can help children to acquire in order to progress towards the Early Learning Goals.

All the games in this book are designed to support the Foundation Stage curriculum and include the Stepping Stones and Early Learning Goals relevant to each game.

Using the games

Early learning activities should be happy and positive experiences. When an adult and child are engaged in a game together, there is a relaxed atmosphere of co-operation. Learning takes place as a natural outcome of a shared experience, not as a thing apart. This approach reflects what we know about the best way for young children to learn. Sharing the game should be an enjoyable time for both adult and child. If a game is not working with your child, it may be that he is just not ready for it at the moment, or that he is simply not in the mood. In this case, try it again in a few weeks or months. When a game is proving successful, always finish on a high note, while your child is still enjoying it. You can always return to it on another day.

The games in this book are set out in an easy-to-use format. The resources needed are all items that are likely to be found in any home or early years setting. Many games are constructed around experiences that are part of the everyday routine of young children.

The adult's role

The influence that an adult has can be summed up in two phrases – 'provide examples' and 'open doors'. Language is made up of two strands: receptive language and expressive language. Receptive language is what a child takes in and what he understands. Expressive language is what a child puts out and what he uses.

To develop good receptive language, children need to hear a wide range of examples of how language is used. An interested adult can play a major role in providing these examples. This does not mean that we should bombard children with a constant stream of talk, but rather that we should talk naturally with them, answering their questions, picking up on their interests and encouraging their curiosity. We can provide models of good speech simply by feeding correct forms back to a child, as part of natural conversation. An adult who responds to the statement 'I've eaten all my dinner' with the comment 'Oh good, you've eaten all of it up', is providing their child with a correct model in an unselfconscious way, allowing learning through trial and error, without negative comment.

In terms of opening doors, the adult's role is firstly to introduce activities and materials that provide a child with opportunities to learn. Choose activities that are at the correct level for your child and ask questions that he can answer either straight away, or with a little help from you. Take an interest in your child's learning discoveries. Your enthusiasm will encourage him to want to take things further. Helping your child to make links between new learning and his overall knowledge is crucial. This skill will stand him in good stead throughout his education, and beyond. Above all, the adult needs to be ready to offer praise for strengths and support for weaknesses.

Daily routines and experiences

Young children do not have an idea of learning as a separate activity that is distinct from their daily routine. Because they possess a natural curiosity, and much of the world is new to them, they are susceptible to learn as they go along. Events and objects that may seem mundane to an adult, can offer endless fascination for them. Once we understand this fact, we can harness it to provide them with a wide range of learning opportunities.

The chapters in this book mirror typical routines in a child's day, making it easy to incorporate the games into everyday activities. With a little imagination and a good deal of enthusiasm, even the most basic daily routine can offer a variety of possibilities for your child to acquire new skills. Some of the games in this book are designed to help you look at daily routines and experiences with a new eye. Once you have begun to see how this works, you will realise that the possibilities are endless.

CHAPTER 1

INDOOR FUN

Between the ages of three and five, children's vocabulary expands rapidly. While the two-and-a-half-year-old will be managing with a vocabulary of approximately 300 words, the five-year-old will have between 1500 and 2000 words at his disposal. At the beginning of this stage of development, your child may still simplify or telescope words. By the end of this phase, he will not only be able to use concrete nouns (words that refer to actual objects) correctly, but will also be showing an interest in, and asking about, the meaning of abstract words (words that refer to feelings and ideas).

BUILDING VOCABULARY

Words are powerful tools. They make it possible for us to organise our thinking. When a child can label an object, she can ask for it, reject it or remember it – she can talk about it when it is not physically present. Each new word that she learns helps her to expand her personal catalogue of the world around her. It is this catalogue – of things that she has seen, people she has met and of feelings and experiences – that make it possible for her to order her thoughts.

Young children are eager to add new words to their vocabulary, and they will seize the opportunity to acquire new labels, if they are given the chance. Patient adult assistance is needed to help young children to expand their vocabulary effectively.

How you can help
● Talk to your child as you carry out simple everyday procedures. If you are helping her to get dressed, name the items of clothing as you do so, saying, 'Let's put on your jeans next'. Talk her through shopping items as you add them to the shopping trolley, and name parts of the body as you bath her.
● Play with words. Make up your own fun, silly labels for things together. Read poems and stories, such as *The Quangle Wangle's Hat* by Edward Lear (Little Mammoth).
● Be patient and answer your child's questions about what things are called. Offer the names for unfamiliar items when you encounter them, even if she does not ask you.
● Enjoy sharing 'naming' books together. Look out for picture books that show a variety of scenes with lots of associated objects in them. Spend time looking at the pictures together and talking about the different things that you can see.

LANGUAGE FOR LEARNING
Beyond the simple name labels for objects, children also need to be able to describe items according to the qualities that they possess. As they learn the words for colour, shape and size, children are learning their first mathematical vocabulary. They add to this when they acquire the names for the numbers. As they describe the

feel and texture of objects, young children are experimenting with early science vocabulary.

When they move into the more formal setting of school, children will also encounter the abstract, specialised words that we use to describe the thinking processes that we carry out in the act of learning. They will discover that we use words such as 'estimate' in maths, and 'predict' in science, where we might use 'guess' elsewhere.

The broader your child's vocabulary is, and the deeper his understanding is of that vocabulary when he enters school, the easier it will be for him to make the move into that learning environment.

How you can help
● Share books together that promote the learning of descriptive words, such as *Old Hat, New Hat* by Stan and Jan Berenstain (Collins).
● When you and your child are looking at things together, use a varied selection of describing words. Play a game in which you take turns to find a new word to describe an object.
● Help your child to understand more abstract words by linking them, as much as possible, to concrete objects. Make collections of items of the same colour. Let him touch and feel different shapes in the form, for example, things such as cracker biscuits.
● Encourage your child to become familiar with the language that he will hear in the setting. Repeat questions, substituting more specialist words for simpler ones, for example, say, 'Can you guess how many sweets are in the packet?' and 'Can you estimate how many there are?'.

MAKING LINKS
To make their thinking and their learning efficient, children need to 'file' vocabulary in an orderly way. They need to have a sense of words that belong together, for example, to be aware that a kettle, a cooker and a frying pan are all likely to be found in a kitchen; to understand that blue, red and green all say something about the colour of an object, while square, triangular or circular will describe its shape. As children make these links between words, they reinforce a range of ideas or concepts that are vital for effective learning.

Later, they will also need to make other links, to begin to understand the connection between spoken language and the print that they see around them. They need to understand that the group of letters that we see on a label, for example, represents the word that we use to name the item. It is essential to be able to make links in their thinking, if children are to begin to understand how the world works.

How you can help
● Reinforce your child's understanding of things that belong together by playing a game where you name a word, and she has to say a word that is linked to it, for example, 'Knife and… (fork); fish and… (chips)'.
● Draw your child's attention to labels on goods in shops. Show her that, in supermarkets, the labels on the aisles tell us what sort of things we will find in that part of the shop. Point out labels on lorries and vans and explain how they help us to know what these vehicles might be carrying.
● Have fun with labels. Pretend that everything in the room is for sale. Make labels to stick on each item. Take it in turns to be the 'salesperson' and to explain to the 'customer' what everything is.

LEARNING OPPORTUNITY
● To learn the vocabulary of colour and size.

YOU WILL NEED
Pile of washing in an assortment of colours, with some items, such as socks, in a variety of sizes.

 STEPPING STONE Build up vocabulary that reflects the breadth of their experiences.

EARLY LEARNING GOAL Communication, language and literacy: Extend their vocabulary, exploring the meanings and sounds of new words.

Pair it

Sharing the game
● Explain to your child that the washing needs to be sorted out before it can be put away, and ask him to help you.
● Suggest that you start by sorting the clothes into piles of the same colour. Choose a colour and ask him to find all the items in that colour and put them together. Work alongside your child, saying, for example, 'I've found a blue sock. What have you found that is blue?'.
● When you have found all of the items in one colour, work through other colours, until all the clothes are sorted.
● Explain that you need to put the pairs of socks together, making sure that both socks in a pair are the same size. As you work through a pile, compare the socks with one another, using phrases such as 'too big', 'too long' and 'too small'. Encourage your child to place socks side by side, and to lay them on top of each other.

Taking it further
● Talk about dark and light shades of the same colour as you sort out the washing.
● Sort the clothes into dark and light colours.
● Draw circles of colour on to small pieces of card. Hold up a card and ask your child to find an article of clothing of that colour and to put it on. Ask him to name the colour that he is looking for, and to say whether the item is too big, too small or too long for him.

LEARNING OPPORTUNITY
● To learn the vocabulary that describes the texture of objects.

YOU WILL NEED
Objects with different textures.

 STEPPING STONE Extend vocabulary, especially by grouping and naming.

 EARLY LEARNING GOAL Communication, language and literacy: Extend their vocabulary, exploring the meanings and sounds of new words.

Touch and tell

Sharing the game
● Tell your child that you are going to play a game in which you describe something in the room. Explain that you are going to talk about how the object feels rather than what it looks like.
● Choose an appropriate item to describe, so that you can model for your child what you would like her to do. Run your fingers over the object as you try to find as many words as you can to tell your child how it feels. Invite your child to feel the item too, and to say if she agrees with the words that you have chosen.

● Tell your child that it is her turn to tell you how something in the room feels. Help her by asking questions such as, 'Does it feel smooth or rough?' and 'Is it soft or hard?'.
● As you move around the room to new objects, try to introduce as many different texture words as you can such as crinkly, twisted, furry, silky, bumpy, prickly, stubbly and so on.

Taking it further
● Play an opposites game. Touch something hard and tell your child, 'I've found something hard, so you find something soft to touch'.
● Make 'touch' collections. Ask your child to fetch items that are smooth to put on a plate, and items that are bumpy to put on a piece of bubble wrap, and so on.

YOU WILL NEED
Pieces of paper; pencils.

STEPPING STONE
Extend vocabulary, especially by grouping and naming.

EARLY LEARNING GOAL
Communication, language and literacy: Extend their vocabulary, exploring the meanings and sounds of new words.

Count down

Sharing the game

● Tell your child that you are going to play a counting game. Explain that you are going to count as many different things as you can that you can see around you.

● Give your child a piece of paper and a pencil. Explain that you are going to take it in turns to count something, and that you will go first, to show him exactly what to do.

● Say, 'I am going to count the pans in the cupboard'. Draw a pan on the piece of paper. Then go to the cupboard and count the pans. As you say each number, put marks in a row on the paper, next to the drawing of the pan. Count the marks again, touching each one with the pencil nib as you count.

● Invite your child to choose something to count. Help him to draw the picture, if necessary. Let him count his chosen objects, joining in if he needs your help.

● Aim for variety in the things that you count, for example, buttons on coats, spoons in the drawer, windows in the room, toys in the box and so on.

Taking it further

● Place piles of small objects on a table, such as buttons, paper clips, macaroni and shells. Give your child an empty egg-box. Ask him to put certain numbers of the objects into each section. Say, for example, 'Can you count six buttons into this section?'.

● Use a felt-tipped pen to number the sections in the egg-box from 1 to 12. Point to and say each numeral in turn, and ask your child to count the correct number of shells and so on into that section.

LEARNING
OPPORTUNITY
● To learn the language
of shape.

YOU WILL NEED
Collection of shopping
items including cans,
boxes, packets and
plastic bottles; pieces of
paper; pencil.

 STEPPING STONE
Extend vocabulary,
especially by grouping
and naming.

★ EARLY LEARNING
GOAL
Communication,
language and literacy:
Extend their vocabulary,
exploring the meanings
and sounds of new
words.

Unpack and stack

Sharing the game

● Tell your child that you are going to play a sorting game. Draw a circle on one piece of paper, a square on another, a rectangle on a third and a triangle on a fourth. As you draw each shape, name it and talk about it with your child. Show her that a circle has no corners, all the sides of a square are exactly the same and so on.

● Lay the pieces of paper out on the table in a row. Pick up a food can and explain that you are going to look at it carefully to see if you can spot one of the shapes that you have drawn. Trace your finger around the circular end of the can, saying, 'Look, here's a circle. This belongs by the paper with the circle on it.'

● Ask your child to choose an item and to look at it carefully to find a shape. Encourage her to say which shape she can see, and to place the item by the correct piece of paper.

Taking it further

● Let your child dip the bottoms of plastic bottles, empty cotton reels, plastic building bricks and so on into paint to make shape prints. Ask her to tell you the shapes that she has printed.

● Cut different-shaped holes in pieces of paper and place them over pictures cut from magazines. Ask your child to describe the pictures, beginning by saying, for example, 'Through the circle I can see…'.

LEARNING OPPORTUNITY
● To make connections between objects and the purposes for which they are used.

YOU WILL NEED
Selection of cutlery: knife, fork, soupspoon, dessertspoon, teaspoon, tablespoon; selection of crockery: dinner plate, bowl, cup and saucer, side plate, mug and glass.

 STEPPING STONE
Begin to make patterns in their experience through grouping.

EARLY LEARNING GOAL
Communication, language and literacy: Use talk to organise ideas.

Soup spoons

Sharing the game

● Explain to your child that you are going to play a game about laying the table. Show him the cutlery and crockery, naming each item as you do so.

● Tell your child that you are going to name some things that you would like to eat. Ask him to put the cutlery that you will need to eat that particular food on the table. Encourage him to name the cutlery as he puts it on the table.

● Tell your child what you are going to eat first, for example, 'I think that today I will have some soup'. Ask him to lay the table for you.

● Work through a variety of different foods and drinks, including things such as 'a cup of coffee with sugar' and 'some jelly from the big bowl', to encourage your child to think about the names of different spoons.

Taking it further

● Cut some pictures of foods from magazines and put them on the table, with the incorrect items of crockery and cutlery beside them. Ask your child to sort out the correct items.

● Let your child choose the foods. Offer silly suggestions, such as a fork to go with soup, and ask him to explain to you why you are wrong and what would be the correct choice.

LEARNING OPPORTUNITY
● To think about how one thing may be linked to another.

YOU WILL NEED
Collection of household objects that have come from different rooms (or a collection of items that come from different storage spaces). Include some things that could belong in more than one place, such as a bar of soap (the kitchen or the bathroom).

STEPPING STONE
Use talk to connect ideas.

EARLY LEARNING GOAL
Communication, language and literacy: Use talk to organise thinking.

Tidy-up time

Sharing the game
● Show your child the collection of items and say that you are going to help each other to sort them all out and put them back in the correct places.
● Pick up the first item and ask your child where she thinks it has come from. When she has made a suggestion, ask why she thought that this was the correct place. Suggest that you make piles of things that belong in the same place.
● Work through all the different objects in the collection. Ask your child each time why she has suggested that particular place to tidy away the item.
● With objects that could belong in more than one place, encourage your child to suggest more than one answer, and to give a reason for each one.

Taking it further
● Ask your child to help you to sort the shopping. Encourage her to sort out, for example, the foods that need to be kept cold, cleaning items and so on.
● Collect together as many pairs of shoes as possible and jumble them up. Play a game of sorting them into pairs, and talk about colours, size and patterns.

LEARNING OPPORTUNITY
● To learn the language of maths – number words and phrases such as 'more than' and 'less than'.

YOU WILL NEED
Teapot; cup; piece of paper; pencil.

STEPPING STONE
Talk activities through, reflecting on and modifying what they are doing.

EARLY LEARNING GOAL
Communication, language and literacy: Use talk to clarify thinking and ideas.

How many?

Sharing the game
● Tell your child that you are going to play a guessing game.
● Help your child to fill the teapot with water, encouraging him to look at how much water goes into the pot.
● Show your child the cup and ask him to guess how many cups of water he thinks that he can pour from the teapot. Ask questions such as, 'Do you think it will be about two cups?' and 'Do you think it will be as many as ten cups?'.

● Draw a row of tally marks on the piece of paper, equal to the number that your child has suggested.
● Ask your child to pour some cups of water. Count with him as he fills the cup. Let him cross off a mark for each cup that he pours. If he runs out of tally marks, ask him to add one more for each extra cup that he pours.
● When the teapot is empty, look at the paper together. Ask your child whether there were more cups of water than he guessed, or less.

Taking it further
● Use a tube of sweets, varying the number of sweets that you leave in the tube. Let your child feel the weight of the tube, and shake it a little, before he guesses the number of sweets inside.
● Ask your child to guess how many toys he can pack away in a box in one minute. Time him and then count the toys with him to check if he was correct.
● Explain that we use a special word called 'estimate' for a guess that we are going to check.

LEARNING OPPORTUNITY
● To think through why things are happening, and to make suggestions about what might happen if particular changes are made.

YOU WILL NEED
Three dirty plates (preferably greasy); washing-up bowl; dishcloth; cold and hand-hot water; washing-up liquid.

 STEPPING STONE
Use talk to connect ideas, explain what is happening and anticipate what might happen next.

 EARLY LEARNING GOAL
Communication, language and literacy: Use talk to clarify thinking and ideas.

Washing well

Sharing the game
● Explain to your child that you are trying to find the best way to get the dirty dishes clean. Show her the dirty plates and ask her to help you with some experiments.
● Ask your child to fill the bowl with cold water and to wash the first plate by wiping the dishcloth over it. Look at the plate with her, asking if she thinks that it looks really clean.

● Now fill the bowl with hand-hot water, and ask your child to wash the second plate in the same way. Ask if she thinks that this plate will be cleaner or not. Encourage her to compare the two plates.
● Before adding washing-up liquid to the water, ask your child if she thinks that this will make any difference. Let her wash the third plate and compare all three to check which is the cleanest.

Taking it further
● Half-fill two glasses with hand-hot water. Drop a small blob of cooking oil into each. Show your child how the oil stays in one blob on top of the water.
● Drip some washing-up liquid into one glass. Stir the water in both glasses. Show your child how the oil is now in lots of small blobs. Ask if she thinks the oil will run back into one big blob in both glasses. Watch with her.
● Explain that the washing-up liquid breaks up the oil, which makes it easier to wash it off plates.

LEARNING OPPORTUNITY
● To learn to write their own name and other common words.

YOU WILL NEED
Pieces of card, approximately 5cm by 10cm; pencils; felt-tipped pens or crayons.

 STEPPING STONE Ascribe meanings to marks.

 EARLY LEARNING GOAL
Communication, language and literacy: Write their own names and other things such as labels.

Name it!

Sharing the game
● Suggest to your child that he help you to make some labels to put on the table so that everyone knows where they should sit.
● As your child watches you, write his name clearly on a piece of paper. Write one letter at a time, talking about the movements that you are making as you write. Ask him to copy the letter on to one of the cards, helping him if

necessary. Work through each letter of his name, making sure that he watches and listens as you explain how you are forming each letter. When his name is complete, let him decorate the edges of the card.
● Repeat the process again with the names of other members of the family, or of the group.
● Ask your child to put the cards out carefully around the table in the correct places.
● Suggest that your child might like to label other things around the house or room. Make a few name labels at a time and attach them with Blu-Tack to chairs, coat pegs and so on.

Taking it further
● Help your child to set up a tea party for his toys and to make place names for them.
● Make other labels to attach to everyday items around the room. Occasionally, take the labels away when your child is not looking. Pretend that there is a mystery character that keeps removing the labels. Ask your child to sort them out and to put them back in the correct places.

LEARNING OPPORTUNITY
● To experiment with words in the telling of stories.

YOU WILL NEED
At least five family and toy name cards from the game 'Name it!' on page 19.

 STEPPING STONE
Begin to be aware of the way stories are structured.

 **EARLY LEARNING GOAL**
Communication, language and literacy: Explore and experiment with words.

What happened next?

Sharing the game
● Explain to your child that you are going to make up a story together, and that lots of people she knows will be in this story.
● Shuffle the family and toy name cards and place them face-down on the table.
● Begin to tell a story with the opening, 'One day, when the wind was howling in the trees outside, and the rain was beating on the window…'.
● Ask your child to pick up a name card. Weave the name into the story, by saying, for example, 'Jack sat indoors feeling very sad because he had nothing to do. Suddenly…'.
● Pause again and pick up another card. Continue with, 'Aaron burst into the room and said…'. Invite your child to complete the sentence. Continue the story, picking up your child's idea. Pause every now and then to pick up a card and add that person into the story. Let your child contribute parts of the story, until all the cards have been used.

Taking it further
● Tell traditional stories, such as 'Goldilocks and the Three Bears', and let your child join in. Substitute the traditional characters with family or toy names, choosing them by asking your child to turn over the cards as above, to create an amusing story.
● Let your child tell increasingly more of the story once you have included the first name.

LEARNING OPPORTUNITY
● To understand that information can be conveyed in the form of written language.

YOU WILL NEED
Flour; margarine; grated cheese; water; cups to measure ingredients; mixing bowl; rolling-pin; the recipe on page 128.

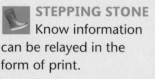

STEPPING STONE
Know information can be relayed in the form of print.

EARLY LEARNING GOAL
Communication, language and literacy: Know that print carries meaning and, in English, is read from left to right and top to bottom.

Look and cook

Sharing the game
● Invite your child to help you to do some baking in the kitchen. Explain that you will need to follow a recipe.
● Look at the recipe together. Cover up the words in the recipe, and ask your child how much the pictures tell you about what he needs and what you should do.
● Explain to your child that the words on the page will help him to know exactly what you will need to make the cheese straws. Tell him that in a recipe we call the food things that we need the 'ingredients'. Say that the words also tell you exactly what you must do.

● Read out the list of ingredients and collect them together.
● Then read each step of the recipe in turn, talking about how the pictures and the words together help you to understand what to do. Encourage your child to do as much as possible, but help when it becomes necessary.

Taking it further
● Talk about the things that are not clear from the recipe, for example, how much water to add.
● Point out that it does not say how big to make the cheese straws. Talk about whether they should be thick or thin, long or short. Say that the bigger the cheese straws are, the longer they will take to cook, so it would be better not to make them too big and thick.
● Ask your child to suggest what could have been written down to make things clearer.

LEARNING OPPORTUNITY
● To learn to recognise and read some common words.

YOU WILL NEED
A small cardboard box such as a shoebox; paper; pen; sticky tape.

 STEPPING STONE
Begin to recognise some familiar words.

EARLY LEARNING GOAL
Communication, language and literacy: Read a range of familiar and common words.

Treasure trail

Sharing the game
● Tell your child that you are going to play a treasure-hunt game. Explain that, first, she needs to know how to read the clues.
● Write the word 'on' on a piece of paper, and tape it to the top of the cardboard box. Say that you have taped it on the box to remind her what the word is. Do the same with the words 'in' and 'under', taping

them inside and underneath the box. Write the word 'look' on a piece of paper and draw two eyes beside it. Tell your child what the word is.
● Now go to lay the trail, leaving your child to look at the words. Hide a small 'treasure'. Write a note, for example, 'look on the table'. Keep it to give to your child. Put a note on the table saying 'look in the cupboard'. Leave a trail of approximately five notes, using the words 'look in/on/under the…' leading to the treasure.
● Give your child the first note. Let her try to read the words that you have prepared with her and help with the final word. Do this with each note, until she finds the treasure.

Taking it further
● Label the places where your child will be looking for the treasure with their names. Encourage her to look at these labels to try to read the whole clue herself.
● Write the words 'not here' on a card, together with a cross. Add this to the beginning of each of the clues, except the first one.

CHAPTER 2

THE WORLD OUTSIDE

For young children, learning is not a separate activity that takes place in a specialist setting. Different environments hold the potential for young children to learn different skills, and the broader the opportunities offered to them, the wider and sounder their learning is likely to be. Even the most everyday of excursions can lend itself to numerous learning opportunities. With help, children can be encouraged to use their curiosity as a starting-point for practising a variety of language skills, such as acquiring new vocabulary, formulating questions, and early reading and writing.

PUTTING LEARNING INTO CONTEXT

The purpose of any learning is to prepare, in one way or another, for real life. If young children are given the opportunity to see how the things that they do at home or in an early years setting relate to the outside world, they will view learning as a practical, purposeful activity, and they will be encouraged to engage fully in the learning process. Likewise, if they are allowed to bring their observations from the outside world into the learning situation, they will view the learning environment as significant and relevant. Children, who have a positive attitude towards learning, will receive the full benefit from it. Since language is the tool that we use for learning, opportunities to utilise a variety of language skills in different contexts will be invaluable.

How you can help

● Provide your child with practical opportunities to use her skills. Let her ask for a few items when you are shopping. Give your child her own small amount of money to spend on a shopping trip.

● Help your child to make links between what she sees in the outside world and activities that she has carried

out. When watching a builder laying bricks, remind her of her own attempts to find the correct mixture of sand and water to make sand pies. Talk about what would happen if the builder's cement was too wet and sloppy.

● Encourage your child to tell her friends and relatives about any outing that she has been on.

● Let your child sign her name or add a picture to letters that you are writing to your friends and relatives.

● Suggest that your child share a book that she knows well with a younger sibling or friend, relating the story to the younger child.

PROVIDING WIDER LEARNING EXPERIENCES

While trips to distant places can add interest and a new excitement to young children's learning, it is important to remember that, for a young child, the wider world can mean anything from the back garden to the local park. The most ordinary excursion can offer real opportunities to practise a variety of language skills if it is approached in the correct way. You can also provide children with an experience of the wider world by inviting people from outside their world to talk with them.

How you can help

● As you take your child to the shops or the park, describe the things that you can see.

● Create a renewed sense of interest for your child in things around him, for example, by pretending to be a visitor from space. Ask about everyday items and places, as if you know nothing about them.

● Go out with your child in all weathers. Rather than regarding a wet day as a nuisance, dress up just for the purpose of going out to see, feel and taste the rain. Look at raindrops on different leaves. See which things get soggy and which throw off the rain. Encourage your child to look, touch and talk.

● Ask an older friend or family member to tell your child about his or her childhood. Encourage your child to compare the story with his own experiences.

● Invite visitors from other countries or cultures to talk to your child about events or customs that are special and important to them.

ENCOURAGING CURIOSITY

Far from being a negative characteristic, curiosity is the positive drive that lies behind a great deal of real learning. In young children, the desire to find out why or how something happens provides them with a sense of purpose and an excitement in the learning situation. Children who ask questions have a mind that is open to new information. The ability to ask appropriate, informed questions is a skill to be fostered if we want young children to be ideally receptive to learning.

How you can help

● Try to listen to your child's questions and to respond to them. If it really is an inconvenient time, always hold the door open for her to return with the question. Say, 'It is a little bit difficult for me to answer that properly just now, and I do want to answer you properly. Could you ask me again in a moment, when I'm not quite so busy?'.

● Try to make time simply to be around for your child to talk to.

● On everyday outings, build in time to just stop, look and listen. Talk with your child about what she can see around her. Encourage her to look in detail at things.

● Provide a good model by asking questions yourself when you are in your child's company. For example, if you are at a museum, ask the guide about a picture or exhibit that interests you. Ask the greengrocer how early he has to get up to collect the fruit and vegetables.

● Help your child to seek out answers to questions, such as from the local library, by asking people who might know or by looking on the Internet.

● Let your child see that you are interested and curious about the world around you. Look closely at it yourself.

● Enjoy making up questions that do not have obvious or even possible answers, for example, 'How many stars are there in the sky?', 'How many drops of water does it take to make a cloud?' and so on.

● Do not always jump in with questions for your child in an eager attempt to make the most of a learning opportunity. Let her natural curiosity take the lead now and then.

LEARNING OPPORTUNITY
● To talk confidently about what they are doing and to use the language of comparison.

YOU WILL NEED
Earth or sand; water; aprons; plastic spade; plastic bucket; different-sized containers.

STEPPING STONE
Use a widening range of words to express or elaborate ideas.

EARLY LEARNING GOAL
Communication, language and literacy: Speak clearly and audibly with confidence and control.

Mud-pie magic

Sharing the game
● Ask your child if he knows the best way to make mud or sand pies. Is it better to use a lot of sand and a little bit of water, or a little bit of sand and a lot of water? Suggest that he try to find out.

● Start off by encouraging your child to use just a small amount of water. Let him feel the sand, and ask if it feels crumbly or mushy. Invite him to try to make a pie with it. If the pie does not stay together, ask what he thinks made it 'collapse'.

● Now let your child experiment with more water. Encourage him to do so with some sand that has been shovelled away from the rest, so that he still has drier sand to work with later. Ask if the sand is wetter now. Does it feel sloppier? Will it make a better pie?

● As your child works with the sand, encourage him to compare one pie with another, and to comment on why things are happening. Suggest that he use different-sized containers, and ask which pie is bigger or smaller than another, and which one is biggest or smallest.

Taking it further
● Encourage your child to build pies in a row with increasing quantities of water, and to judge the best one.
● Suggest that he make a row of pies, with each one slightly bigger than the last.
● Ask which sand is better to work with – crumblier, drier sand or damper, squidgier sand?

Rubbings walk

Sharing the game

● Invite your child to join you in creating some pattern pictures. Explain that she is not going to draw the patterns, but that she is going to 'find' them outside.

● Go outside and look for a wall or a path that is textured, but not so rough as to make rubbing difficult. Ask your child to feel the surface, and talk about how it feels. Use four small lumps of Blu-Tack to attach a piece of paper to the surface of the wall or path and ask your child to choose a colour from the wax crayons.

● Now show your child how to rub hard with the crayon over the paper. Talk about the pattern of the wall or path as it appears.

● When the pattern is showing clearly, try a different surface. Look for manhole covers in paths, embossed paving stones, tree trunks and so on.

● As your child makes rubbings from different surfaces, introduce words such as grooved, ridged, lumpy and so on. Look at the resulting patterns and talk about them being mottled, blotchy, stripy or zigzags.

Taking it further

● Trim the rubbings into brick shapes. Help your child to paste them on to a large sheet of paper and make a house. As she works, ask which brick she is going to add next, encouraging her to describe the pattern on the brick of her choice.

LEARNING OPPORTUNITY
● To use a widening range of words to describe textures and patterns.

YOU WILL NEED
Lots of small sheets of paper; coloured wax crayons; Blu-Tack.

STEPPING STONE
Use a widening range of words to express or elaborate ideas.

EARLY LEARNING GOAL
Communication, language and literacy: Speak clearly and audibly with confidence and control.

LEARNING OPPORTUNITY
● To learn the vocabulary of shape.

YOU WILL NEED
Trip to the shops or any outing.

 STEPPING STONE Build up vocabulary that reflects the breadth of their experiences.

EARLY LEARNING GOAL
Communication, language and literacy: Extend their vocabulary, exploring the meanings and sounds of new words.

Spot a shape

Sharing the game
● Play this game with your child as you are walking to and around the shops, or on any trip out. Ask your child if he would like to play an 'I spy' game.
● Now explain that you are going to choose a shape and your child has to see how many things he can spot of that shape.
● Say to him, for example, 'Let's start with a circle and see what we can find that

has the shape of a circle. Look at the wheels on that car. What shape are they?'.
● Prompt your child into seeing a few circular-shaped things in this way and then let him try for himself. You may wish to keep a few possibilities in mind to help him, such as street lights, coins, the sun, balls, street signs, clocks and so on.
● Choose another shape and start again, for example, square shapes – windows, houses, paving stones, signs and so on; rectangles – doors, windows, trucks, books, blocks of flats, newspapers, cereal boxes, greetings cards and so on; triangles – road signs, car stickers, roofs, some garden trees and so on.

Taking it further
● Encourage your child to look at various items around the house from different angles to see if the shape of them is always the same.
● Cut out pictures of circular-shaped items from magazines and stick them on to a large sheet of paper cut into a circle. Do the same with items of other shapes.

LEARNING OPPORTUNITY
● To learn new vocabulary through observation and experience.

YOU WILL NEED
Outside area where a variety of plants and shrubs are growing; magnifying glass (optional).

STEPPING STONE
Build up vocabulary that reflects the breadth of their experiences.

EARLY LEARNING GOAL
Communication, language and literacy: Extend their vocabulary, exploring the meanings and sounds of new words.

Up close

Sharing the game

● Ask your child if she would like to be an explorer with you. Explain that explorers try to look at things very carefully and closely. If you have a magnifying glass, show your child how it makes the smallest detail very clear when you look through it. Say that you are going to go on an expedition together.

● Once outside, explain that you are going to 'investigate' plant stems first. Find a plant and ask your child to look very carefully at the stem. Ask her if it is smooth or hairy, or whether it has thorns. Does the stem look straight or curved, stiff or bendy?

● Now find another plant and compare it to the first. Look at the stems of several plants, including shrubs.

● Look at leaves, discussing whether they are shiny or dull and whether the edges are smooth or jagged. Encourage your child to talk about the different shapes – are they more round or oval, thin or pointed? Let her gently feel them. Are they soft, leathery or feathery? Do they feel smooth or rough?

● Look at and feel the bark on trees. Use words such as 'bumpy' and 'knobbly', 'rough' and 'smooth' to describe it.

● Walk around the area, looking in detail, talking about and comparing anything and everything.

Taking it further

● Encourage your child to record her observations with drawings. Add captions for her and put her work together as a book, with the title 'The day I explored plants, by (*your child's name*)'.

LEARNING OPPORTUNITY
● To ask questions based on observations.

YOU WILL NEED
Just you and your child.

Wondering walk

Sharing the game

● Choose a time to play this game when you are not in a hurry. Tell your child that you are going out for a walk, but that you do not know yet where you are going. Say that it is a 'wondering' walk, adding, 'I wonder where we will end up?'.

● Set off at a leisurely pace, encouraging your child to look at the things around him and listen carefully to any sounds. Help him to

start thinking about what he can see and hear by saying, 'I wonder what made that noise?' or 'I wonder where that woodlouse is going?'.

● At junctions, say, for example, 'I wonder which way we should go next? Where do you think that road would lead us to?' or 'I wonder what is happening over there, where those men are working on the road. Shall we go that way and see?'.

● Explain to your child that, when we are in a hurry, we do not always have time to look around us properly and think about what is going on. Say that today there is plenty of time to look and wonder about things.

● When your child has grasped the idea of looking around and asking questions about what he can see, draw his attention to things that will really make him think. Say, for example, 'Look at that plant growing from the top of the wall. I wonder how it got there?'. Show pleasure in the questions that your child wonders about as well as answers that he suggests.

Taking it further

● Play 'I wonder' at home, using really good 'wondering' questions, such as, 'I wonder how a worm finds its way underground?'. Ask other family members if there are questions that they wonder about.

STEPPING STONE
Question why things happen, and give explanations.

EARLY LEARNING GOAL
Communication, language and literacy: Enjoy listening to and using spoken language.

LEARNING OPPORTUNITY
● To understand how stories can be built up around a character or an event.

YOU WILL NEED
Small toy vehicles, particularly those seen on a building site; small piles of lentils, butter beans and pasta penne; a few lengths of spaghetti; teaspoons; small-world people; large tray.

 STEPPING STONE
Describe main story settings, events and principal characters.

EARLY LEARNING GOAL
Communication, language and literacy: Enjoy listening to and using spoken and written language, and readily turn to it in their play and learning.

Men at work

Sharing the game
● This is an ideal game to play when you have spent time with your child watching men working on a building site.

● Suggest to your child that she might like to make her own building site. Provide her with a tray and explain that this is the building site. Put a small pile of lentils on the tray, telling her that this is the cement for the builders. Offer the butter beans as paving slabs, the pasta penne as pipes and the spaghetti as cables. Give her the teaspoons to use as spades.

● Encourage your child to fetch the toy vehicles and the small-world people who work on the building site.

● Now say that you would like to know the story of what is happening. Ask who is in charge of the work and encourage your child to name one small-world person as the 'boss'.

● Enquire about the other workers and ask what they are building. Say, 'Can you tell me the story of a day on the building site?'.

Taking it further
● Create other small-world play scenarios to build on your child's experiences. Follow up a visit to the swimming pool, using a bowl as the pool and small-world people as the swimmers. Use soft toys to recreate a visit to the country. Perhaps visit a museum with your child, then make your own. Encourage your child to act as storyteller and describe the scene.

LEARNING OPPORTUNITY
● To listen carefully, and to respond to instructions.

YOU WILL NEED
A small toy to hide; outside area; chair; cardboard box; washing-up bowl.

STEPPING STONE
Respond to simple instructions.

EARLY LEARNING GOAL
Communication, language and literacy: Sustain attentive listening, responding to what they have heard by relevant actions.

Left, right, turn around

Sharing the game
● Place the chair, cardboard box and upturned washing-up bowl around the outside area. Hide the small toy behind a bush, inside the cardboard box, or underneath the upturned bowl.

● Explain to your child that you have hidden a toy. Say that, instead of just asking him to look for it, you will give directions to help him find it. Tell him to listen very carefully and do exactly what you say.

● Begin to give instructions, one at a time, for your child to move around the space. Tell him how many steps to move forwards, left or right. Hold out the appropriate arm to help him with these latter two instructions.

● Do not take your child directly to the hidden toy, but talk him around, over or past the objects that you have placed, or any others that are present in the space. Give instructions to move backwards and sideways, as well as forwards.

● Make sure that your child is within reach of the hidden toy after five or six instructions have been carried out. Call out, 'There!' and ask him to look very carefully around him.

● Hide the toy somewhere else, and play again, giving a different set of instructions.

Taking it further
● Give two instructions at a time, and when your child is competent with this, try three. Make sure that you do not give more instructions than he can remember at once, and do not exceed three.

LEARNING
OPPORTUNITY
● To write a list to serve
as a reminder.

YOU WILL NEED
Paper; pencil.

STEPPING STONE
Ascribe meanings
to marks.

EARLY LEARNING
GOAL
Communication,
language and literacy:
Attempt writing for
different purposes.

Let's go shopping

Sharing the game

● This game is best played before a real shopping trip, but, if this is not possible, make it part of playing a shopping game. Explain to your child that it is hard to remember everything that you need to buy at the shops, so you are going to write a shopping list to help you. Suggest that she might like to have one too, so that she can help with the shopping.

● If you are making the list for a real shopping trip, consider letting your child add at least one item of her own choice. If you are playing a shopping game, let her imagination be the inspiration for the list.

● Write the shopping list together. Name each item clearly, emphasising the first sound in the word, then spell out the word as you write it. Beside the word, draw a small picture of the item, or let your child contribute the drawing. Explain that the drawing will help her to read the word, so that she will remember what to look for in the shop, or what to ask for.

● When you are shopping, or playing 'Shops', let your child have control of the list. Encourage her to look at the picture, then point to the accompanying word and ask her, 'So, what does this word on our list say?'.

Taking it further

● Let your child write the initial letters of words on the list, then you add the rest.

● Help your child to make a list of the characters from story-books that she would like to invite to her birthday party, and let her illustrate it with her drawings.

LEARNING OPPORTUNITY
● To recognise numbers in the environment and to understand their significance.

YOU WILL NEED
Area with houses, shops and traffic.

STEPPING STONE
Show interest in print in the environment.

EARLY LEARNING GOAL
Communication, language and literacy: Know that print carries meaning.

Number walks

Sharing the game
● Go for a walk with your child where there are shops and traffic.
● Ask your child if he has noticed that there are lots of numbers written all around us. Suggest that you play a game by trying to spot numbers and working out what they tell you.
● Draw your child's attention to the number on a house door. Ask him how he thinks that the number might help a visitor, or the postman.
● Encourage your child to look around for other numbers. Explain how car numbers help to keep track of who owns a car. Look at telephone numbers on vans and talk about the purpose of these.

● If your child is finding it difficult to spot numbers, give him some clues. Each time you do this, offer him the chance to tell you what the meaning of the numbers is.
● In shops, ask your child why there are numbers on price labels. Point out the aisle numbers in supermarkets, explaining how these make it easier to find things.
● Notice speed limit signs and talk about how important they are.
● Look at magazines in shops and point out the page numbers. Explain how these help us to find quickly what we want to read.

Taking it further
● Choose a simple non-fiction book on a subject that interests your child, and use the page numbers in the index to look up information with him.
● Find your number in the telephone book with your child and explain to him how it would help people to phone you.

LEARNING OPPORTUNITY
● To realise that print is all around us, and that it conveys information.

YOU WILL NEED
A handful of beads, paper clips or counters; paper bag.

STEPPING STONE
Show interest in print in the environment.

EARLY LEARNING GOAL
Communication, language and literacy: Know that print carries meaning.

Here, there, everywhere

Sharing the game
● Tell your child that you are going to go on a walk. Before you go, ask your child where we usually find words written down. When she has answered, suggest that she might be surprised at the number of different places around us where we can see words. Suggest that you go on a word hunt together.
● Go for a walk and explain to your child

that you would like her to look for words in as many different places as she can. Tell her that each time she spots a different place, you will give her a counter to drop into her paper bag.
● Start by pointing out some print that you have noticed. Explain what information you get from the words that you see. When your child notices print somewhere, encourage her to think about the place where she has seen it, and ask what she thinks it may be telling her. Ask appropriate questions, for example, say, 'The sign on the shop door has some days of the week and some times of the day written on it. What do you think we will know if we read that sign?'.
● Encourage your child to look at moving objects, such as vans and lorries, and to hunt words at heights other than eye level.
● Afterwards, check the number of counters in the bag, to find out in how many different places your child spotted printed words.

Taking it further
● Re-create some of the things that you saw, for example, make a sign to tell people when you are 'open to visitors', and post it on your door, or on your child's bedroom door.

LEARNING OPPORTUNITY
● To use writing to communicate with a friend or relative.

YOU WILL NEED
Paper; pencils; envelopes; stamps.

I wrote a letter

Sharing the game

● Suggest to your child that it would be nice to send a letter to one of his friends, or to a relative such as his grandma. Explain that people enjoy getting letters. Say that you are also going to write a letter while he is writing his. Tell him that you are going to write to someone special.

● Encourage your child to try to put something on paper for his chosen correspondent. This could be a picture, drawn especially for them, a note in pretend writing, or an attempt to write about

something that he has done. Help your child, as appropriate, if he would like you to do so. Write out what he has attempted underneath his writing, helping with spelling, or writing down what he tells you.

● As your child works, try to write a short note to your child, without him seeing his name on it.

● Let him fold his letter and put it in an envelope. Address both letters, letting him see now that your letter is to him. Do not reveal the contents. Invite him to stick the stamps on the envelopes.

● Take your child to a post-box and let him post the letters. Talk about how they will be collected and then taken to be sorted.

● When he is opening his letter from you, remind him that his friend or relative will be enjoying the letter that he sent as well.

Taking it further

● Paint a cardboard box red and cut a slit in it to create a post-box. Make a habit of leaving notes for your child in the box. Ensure that he has access to writing materials to reply.

 STEPPING STONE Use writing as a means of communicating.

EARLY LEARNING GOAL Communication, language and literacy: Write their own names.

LEARNING OPPORTUNITY
● To practise writing their name and attempting other words.

YOU WILL NEED
Paper; pencils; scissors; objects collected on a walk or a trip (these can be as simple as a stone, a leaf, a ticket and so on).

STEPPING STONE
Use writing as a means of recording.

EARLY LEARNING GOAL
Communication, language and literacy: Write their own names and other things such as labels.

My museum

Sharing the game

● Go for a walk with your child and encourage her to collect things that will remind her of where she has been, and what she has seen.

● On your return, suggest that your child might like to make a display of all the things that she found. Explain that the display will be like a museum, with labels to help anyone looking at the objects to know exactly what the things are.

● Offer a display area where the things can safely be left for a few days without needing to be moved. Ask your child to arrange her objects in the way that she thinks looks best.

● Now ask her to write her name on a piece of paper, helping her if necessary. Add an apostrophe and an 's' after her name and help her to write the name of the object, for example, 'Clare's stone'. Accept initial letters only, any attempts at words, or pretend writing. Help with spelling if your child asks you to. Cut around the label, and ask your child to put it with the appropriate object.

● As you write, talk about the various objects, and where they were found, asking your child what made her choose to collect those particular things.

Taking it further

● Write a caption, rather than a simple label. Add a sentence or two about where the object was found, and why your child chose it.

● Encourage her to show her 'museum' to a friend or a family member, and to talk about the labels.

CHAPTER 3

LET'S PRETEND

Between the ages of three and five, children develop an increasing love of stories and acquire the ability to recount recent events and experiences. At this stage, we see them utilising both their own experiences and those that they hear about in stories. 'Make believe' lies at the heart of their play and it enables them to experiment with language. It allows them to 'rehearse' words, phrases and sentence structures that would not otherwise form part of their regular use of language. In their imaginary play, they are able to extend their use of language beyond the limits of their daily experience to prepare themselves for the wider world.

RE-ENACTING STORIES

When children re-enact the stories that they have heard, they draw on the vocabulary and forms of speech that are used in those stories. They experiment with different intonations of voice, appropriate to the characters that they are playing. As they do this, children begin to appreciate that we use different patterns of language in different situations. They realise that it is not only the words we use, but the tone in which we speak and the gestures which accompany our speech, that convey meaning.

How you can help

● Make reading stories a regular part of your routine with your child. Use your local library to access as wide a range of story-books as possible.
● Put expression into reading a story to your child and, if possible, give the various characters in a story different voices.
● Talk about the story afterwards, encouraging your child to remember what happened. Prompt him with questions such as, 'Can you remember what the wolf said then?'.
● Encourage your child to act out the stories that he has heard. Provide some simple props to help. For example, three soft toys, three bowls, three chairs and three cushions will provide all that is needed to act out the story of 'Goldilocks and the Three Bears' (Traditional).
● Let your child take different parts in the stories if he wants to. Be prepared to join in yourself.

BUILDING ON EXPERIENCES

By re-creating their experiences in imaginary play, children are able to practise and reinforce the vocabulary and the language patterns that they have heard in different situations. They may visit a restaurant only once in a while, but by re-creating the scenario in their play, they will strengthen their understanding of the conventions of the speech that we use in such a situation.

Children also like to observe people performing different roles, and then act out those roles. In doing so, they use and acquire an understanding of a broad selection of words that

might not, otherwise, form part of their vocabulary. For example, they begin to make links between certain occupations and particular specialist words and phrases.

How you can help
● Spend time reminiscing about experiences with your child. Have a picnic in the sand-pit following a seaside trip, or re-create a farm that you have visited with model animals.
● Help your child to reinforce new vocabulary by describing things that she saw, and asking if she can remember what they were called.
● Make the most of opportunities provided by situations that your child observes as you are 'out and about'. For example, help her to act out the activities that she has seen taking place on a local building site. Use props that are readily to hand, such as bricks from a construction set, or help to set up 'small-world' play using toy vehicles.

READING AND WRITING IN CONTEXT
Pretend play offers an excellent opportunity for children to learn how reading and writing play a role in many different areas of life. It helps them to understand that these activities are not confined to formal settings such as school, but that literacy is essential for many everyday activities. They can be helped to understand that reading skills are not limited to story-books, but enable people to order food in cafés, look up telephone numbers and so on. Likewise, writing skills are needed to fill in forms and to copy down recipes. Pretend play can provide pleasurable practice in these skills at an appropriate level for your child's current development.

How you can help
● Provide a variety of materials for your child to practise 'writing' during pretend play. Supply notepads and pencils for taking orders in an imaginary restaurant; clipboards and 'charts' for hospital play; potato print stampers and paint; and envelopes, paper and sticker 'stamps' for post-office play. Try to think of writing activities linked to different play scenarios.
● Surround your child with opportunities to experience print and to practise 'reading'. For example, place an old telephone directory in the playhouse, write out a simple menu for a café and put out a recipe book when he is making play-dough cakes.
● Praise all attempts at reading or writing, including pretend reading or 'scribble' writing. With positive reinforcement from you, your child will want to keep practising these skills and will make steady progress towards literacy.

BUILDING CONFIDENCE
As children play together in pretend situations, they practise the phrases that are used in a variety of social situations. Play enables them to try out a range of phrases and language patterns, such as those that we use when we purchase goods in a shop, or make an appointment with a doctor. They know that we vary our language according to the situation and the people we are talking to. When children are given plenty of opportunities for pretend play, they acquire the confidence needed to interact with people other than those they know well. They are more able to start up or respond appropriately to conversation in a variety of different situations. Language skills are crucial not only in

helping them to form friendships, but also in enabling them to function well in the wider world.

How you can help
● Make provision for as wide a range of pretend play as possible. Props need not be elaborate, for example, empty food containers, play money and a bun tin for a till will supply all that is needed for shop play.
● Be prepared, when other children are not available, to play the lesser role in any pretend situation. Allowing your child to be 'in charge' in the role of doctor to your patient, for example, will create confidence.
● Respond positively to your child's performance in the imaginary role. Comment that she sounded just like a real nurse or acted just like a real firefighter.
● Try to provide opportunities for your child to engage in pretend play with other children.

● To use action and some talk to create an imaginary situation, and to learn animal names and the names of animal homes.

YOU WILL NEED
A non-fiction book featuring various animals; chairs or table; old blankets.

 STEPPING STONE
Use action, sometimes with limited talk, that is largely concerned with the 'here and now'.

EARLY LEARNING GOAL
Communication, language and literacy: Use language to imagine and re-create roles and experiences.

Animal's den

Sharing the game
● Share the book with your child and talk about the animals. Point out that animals live in all sorts of places. Explain that some live underground in holes or tunnels, and that some

make dens. Try, if possible, to use different names for animal homes. Say, for example, that we call a badger's home a 'sett' and a rabbit's home a 'warren'.
● Ask your child what sort of animal she would like to be, and what sort of a home she would have.
● Use the chairs or table and blankets to create a den for your child. Encourage her to explore her den and pretend to be her chosen animal. Talk about how the animal would move, when it might come out of its den, what noises it would make and so on.
● Let your child experiment with pretending to be different animals. Make the den smaller or larger, or more like a tunnel, as appropriate.

Taking it further
● Find story-books featuring different types of animals as the main characters. Choose stories such as 'The Three Little Pigs' (Traditional). Ask your child if it would be more fun to pretend to be the wolf or one of the pigs, then act out the story.
● Read 'Little Red Riding Hood' (Traditional) and ask your child which character she would prefer to play.

LEARNING OPPORTUNITY
● To use pretend items to relive and talk about an experience.

YOU WILL NEED
A cardboard box, large enough for your child to fit inside; collection of soft toys or dolls; small pieces of paper, cut to ticket size; coins.

 STEPPING STONE
Use talk, actions and objects to recall and relive past experiences.

EARLY LEARNING GOAL
Communication, language and literacy: Use language to imagine and re-create roles and experiences.

Take a ride

Sharing the game
● After a trip on a bus, suggest to your child that you make his own bus for him to take his toys for a ride. Talk about buying bus tickets and encourage him to help you write prices on the pieces of paper.

● Decide on a bus route together, and place the toys at various 'bus stops' along the route. Make sure that each toy has some coins.

● Give your child the pile of tickets, and tell him to sit in the box ready to drive the bus.

● Push your child to the first stop and help the toys to board the bus.

Encourage him to offer a ticket to the toys in exchange for their coins. Continue along the route, with your child picking up and dropping off passengers as he goes.

Taking it further
● Keep mementoes, such as tickets, leaflets, shells, conkers and so on, from trips out. Make a 'memories' box from an old shoebox to store the items. Play 'Do you remember?' with your child. Take something from the box and ask, 'Do you remember when we collected this?'. Encourage him to retell the story of that particular experience, helping him a little if necessary.

● Use photographs to remind your child about past experiences, and encourage him to retell the events shown in the photos.

LEARNING
OPPORTUNITY

LEARNING OPPORTUNITY
● To use imagination to pretend that everyday objects are something else.

YOU WILL NEED
Cushions; different-coloured buttons; biscuit tin; transparent soft fruit container; piece of elastic; strong sticky tape; empty cereal boxes; string.

 STEPPING STONE Use talk to give new meanings to objects and actions, treating them as symbols for other things.

EARLY LEARNING GOAL
Communication, language and literacy: Use language to imagine and re-create roles and experiences.

Deep-sea diving

Sharing the game
● Ask your child if she would like to come with you, under the sea, to hunt for lost treasure.
● Explain that you need special equipment to go swimming under the sea. Draw flipper shapes on cardboard from the cereal boxes, and cut them out. Make four small holes in the 'flippers' and thread two pieces of string through, to tie the flippers on to your child's feet. Tape the ends of a piece of elastic to each narrow side of the transparent container to hold it in place on your child's head, similar to a diving mask.
● Scatter the cushions on the floor along with some of the buttons. Put the rest in the tin, and hide it under the cushions.
● Encourage your child to 'swim' through the cushions. Draw her attention to the button 'treasure'. Suggest that she hunt under the rocks for more. Let her find the treasure and examine it together. Talk about the different 'jewels' that she has found.

Taking it further
● Create imaginary play environments from large cardboard boxes used to deliver electrical goods. Make a castle by cutting crenellations, or a rocket by covering it with tin foil. Encourage your child to help you, and to choose other household items to serve as appropriate props for a particular game.

● Draw a face on a wooden spoon to make a simple puppet. Let your child hold it in a hand covered with a tea towel, to represent clothes for the puppet.

LEARNING OPPORTUNITY
● To experiment with sounds and words, and to contribute to a story.

YOU WILL NEED
A table; strips of green crêpe paper; cardboard tubes; sticky tape; string; Blu-Tack.

 STEPPING STONE Listen to and join in with stories and poems, one-to-one and also in small groups.

EARLY LEARNING GOAL Communication, language and literacy: Explore and experiment with sounds, words and texts.

In the jungle

Sharing the game

● Attach the strips of crêpe paper to the edges of the table and underneath with Blu-Tack, so that they hang down to form a 'jungle'.
● Ask your child if he would like to come and explore the jungle with you, and to see the jungle animals.
● Suggest that he will need a pair of binoculars to see all the animals.
● Work together to cut two cardboard tubes to the length of

binoculars. Tape the tubes together, then tape a piece of string to the 'binoculars' to make a strap, and hang them around your child's neck.
● Suggest that he creep through the jungle. As he does so, begin a story, using his name. Say, for example, 'Tom was creeping through the jungle, when, suddenly he saw…'. Encourage your child to look through the binoculars and to tell you which animal he can see. Ask him what noise it is making. Add to the story, saying, 'Up behind Tom came creeping a…' and so on.
● If your child has difficulty thinking of animals, help him by describing an animal, asking what it is called and what sound it makes. Include a variety of animals, such as monkeys, hummingbirds, snakes, parrots, tigers and so on.

Taking it further

● Take it in turns to name all sorts of animals, with the other person making its noise, then swap.
● Read one of your child's favourite stories to him, pausing to allow him to add sound effects, when appropriate.

LEARNING OPPORTUNITY
● To practise the language of greetings.

YOU WILL NEED
Two plain paper bags; two cardboard tubes; newspaper; felt-tipped pens; sticky tape; wool; glue.

STEPPING STONE
Begin to use more complex sentences.

EARLY LEARNING GOAL
Communication, language and literacy: Speak clearly and audibly with confidence and control and show awareness of the listener, for example by their use of conventions such as greetings.

Have we met?

Sharing the game
● Ask your child if she would like to help you to make some puppets.
● Give her a paper bag and the felt-tipped pens. Invite her to draw a friendly face on the paper bag. Encourage her to use the middle area of the bag, rather than drawing on the edges.
● Place the cardboard tube in the bag, so that one end protrudes to form a neck. Screw up sheets

of newspaper and ask your child to push them into the bag around the tube. Keep the tube in a central position. When the bag is almost full, gather the open end together and tape it tightly round the tube. Tape down the corners of the bag for a more rounded shape.
● Let your child glue pieces of wool to represent hair on to her puppet, then encourage her to make a friend for it. Repeat the process to make a second puppet.
● Suggest that you pretend that the two puppets have just met, and one wants to be friends with the other. Take one puppet, and give the other to your child. Make your puppet bow slightly to the other, saying, 'Good Morning. Have we met before?'.
● As your child makes her puppet respond, pick up the conversation, trying to include the sort of phrases that we use in social conversation, such as 'Pleased to meet you', 'How are you?', 'Goodbye' and so on.

Taking it further
● Use the puppets to pretend other situations, such as shopkeeper and customer, or teacher and pupil. Encourage your child to vary phrases and greetings according to the situation.

LEARNING OPPORTUNITY
● To develop listening and memory skills.

YOU WILL NEED
Three small items to hide; piece of paper; pencil.

Detectives

Sharing the game

● Invite your child to play a 'hide-and-seek' game with you. Tell him that you are going to pretend that he is a 'detective', who finds things that you have hidden. Tell him that he will have to listen very carefully to know where to look.

● Show your child the three items that you are going to hide. Place the items in obvious places for this first try at the game.

● Return to your child and sit down with the paper and pencil. Pretend to be talking to yourself. Say that you must write down where you have put the things, because you will not remember otherwise. Mention each item in turn and the place where you have put it.

● Challenge your child to find the things, by saying, 'Can you be a detective and find where I put those things?'.

● Hide the items again, making the hiding places a little less obvious this time.

Taking it further

● Make your statements about where the items are hidden a little longer and more challenging. Instead of saying, 'The rubber is in the cupboard', say, 'The rubber is somewhere near the blue vase'.

● Play 'Fetch me three' with your child. Challenge him to go off to different places to fetch three things, but do not name specific items. Ask for something blue from one place, something red from another, and something green from the third place, or ask him to fetch you different-shaped items.

 STEPPING STONE Listen with increasing attention and recall.

EARLY LEARNING GOAL
Communication, language and literacy: Sustain attentive listening, responding to what they have heard by relevant actions.

A day at the beach

Sharing the game
● Lay out all the items near to the sand-pit.
● Explain to your child that you are going to pretend that you are at
the seaside. Say that
you will need help to
get things ready.
● Show your child the
different things that
you have laid out, and
ask her to choose one
thing that she might
take to the beach.
● Encourage your
child to talk to you
about how she would
use that item at the
beach or what it
would be doing
there. Then ask if it
would be a good
idea to pack it into
the bag to use in
your game.

● Continue in this way until there are no items left that are connected
with the beach.
● Take the bag to the sand-pit and unpack all the chosen items with
your child. Set them out to re-create the scene that she has described
and pretend that you are both at the beach.

Taking it further
● Include further items to stimulate discussion, such as a carton of
juice and some sandwiches. Encourage your child to remember and
talk about what she might eat at the seaside.
● Re-create other scenarios. Turn the garden slide into an adventure
park to stimulate memories and talk of a visit there. Use toy animals to
re-create a zoo.

LEARNING OPPORTUNITY
● To talk about a past experience, using the discussion as a stimulus to re-enact it.

YOU WILL NEED
A sand-pit; beach bucket and spade; shells and pebbles (optional); empty plastic drinks bottle; suncream; sun-hat; swimsuit; towel; large bag or basket; several other items not connected with the seaside.

STEPPING STONE
Begin to use talk instead of action to rehearse, reorder and reflect on past experience.

EARLY LEARNING GOAL
Communication, language and literacy: Use language to imagine and re-create roles and experiences.

○ ○

LEARNING
OPPORTUNITY
● To talk about an
imaginary experience.

YOU WILL NEED
Pictures of water scenes
such as lakes, beaches,
swimming pools and so
on, cut from magazines
and travel brochures;
bath or water tray; Blu-
Tack.

 STEPPING STONE
Begin to use talk to
pretend imaginary
situations.

 **EARLY LEARNING
GOAL**
Communication,
language and literacy:
Use talk to organise
ideas.

Water, water

Sharing the game

● Choose one of the pictures that you have cut from a magazine.
Attach it to the wall with Blu-Tack next to the bath, or close to the
water tray.

● When your child is bathing, or playing with the water tray, draw his
attention to the picture. Say, for example, 'I see you're swimming
(playing) in a lake today. Is the water cold?'.

● Continue to talk to your child, as if he is actually present at the
scene in the picture. Ask him why he is there, and how long he is
staying. Encourage him to describe to you how he is feeling as he
enjoys the water.

● Point to different things in the picture and ask your child if he has
noticed them. Create a conversation around them by asking him who
he thinks is on the big boat and whether he would like to climb the
mountain beyond the lake.

● Change the picture on the wall regularly, and help your child to
imagine a new scenario each time.

Taking it further

● Choose other pictures
from magazines with
interesting scenes and help
your child to imagine that
he is there and to tell the
story of what is happening.

● Play 'Imagine if you were
a character from a story'
and ask your child a series
of questions, for example,
'What would you be
wearing?', 'Where would
you be now?', 'What
would you be doing?' and
'Who would be with
you?'. Take it in turns to
ask the questions.

LEARNING OPPORTUNITY
● To learn that marks on paper can have meaning.

YOU WILL NEED
Shoeboxes or cardboard boxes with sides cut lower; small pieces of paper; paper clips; soft toys; plasters; strips of white fabric marked with 'blood' (red felt-tipped pen); lollipop-stick 'thermometer' (with degrees marked in black felt-tipped pen).

 STEPPING STONE Ascribe meanings to marks.

EARLY LEARNING GOAL
Communication, language and literacy: Attempt writing for different purposes.

Does it hurt?

Sharing the game
● Bandage the leg of one of the soft toys with the white fabric and show it to your child. Suggest that the toy needs help and that it might be a good idea to set up a toy hospital.
● Offer your child the shoeboxes to use as beds for the hospital and help her to set up the beds for the toys.
● Attach a piece of paper to the bottom of each box with a paper clip and explain to your child that these 'charts' are used to show if the patients are getting better. Help her to write the name of the

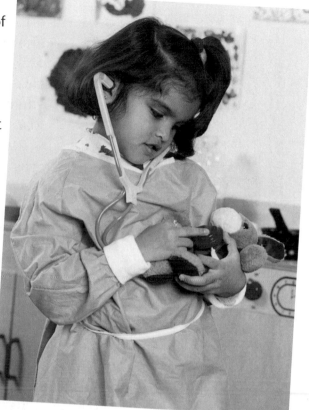

first toy at the top of its chart. Suggest that she take its temperature. Draw a cross on the chart.
● Explain to your child that she should take the toy's temperature later and, if it is hotter, she should write the next cross higher on the paper. If the toy is not as hot, she should write the cross lower down.
● Help to set up more charts for other toys and, as your child adds crosses to the charts, talk about how they show what has been happening to the toy during its stay in hospital.

Taking it further
● Encourage your child to try to add more information to the charts. Suggest that she write the part of the body that is hurt on the chart.
● Help to make a menu for the patients to choose their meals. Let your child contribute drawings, pretend writing, initial letters of words, and so on, according to her current stage of development.

LEARNING OPPORTUNITY
● To use talk to imagine or to re-create an experience, and to learn the language of size and weight.

YOU WILL NEED
Dolls and teddies; set of scales; tape measure; paper; pencils; sticky labels or building blocks (depending on type of scales); Blu-Tack.

 STEPPING STONE
Begin to use talk to pretend imaginary situations.

★ **EARLY LEARNING GOAL**
Communication, language and literacy: Use language to imagine and re-create roles and experiences.

The baby clinic

Sharing the game

● Invite your child to help you set up a 'clinic' to check how well the toys are growing.

● Draw a centimetre rule on a large piece of paper. Attach it to the base of a wall or door with Blu-Tack to form a height chart.

● Set up the scales. Have building blocks ready to use as weights, or sticky labels if you are using scales with a needle.

● Suggest that your child weigh each toy in turn. Help him to keep a record, by writing the toy's name on a piece of paper, and letting him draw a square beside it for each block 'weight' that he uses. On scales with a needle, make small name stickers, to place at the correct mark for each toy. As your child weighs the toys, encourage comparison, talking about which are heavier and lighter.

● Invite your child to measure the toys. Encourage him to stand them against the centimetre rule, and help him to write each toy's name at the correct height, or provide a name sticker for him to put in place. Let him make comparisons and talk about taller and shorter toys.

Taking it further

● Help your child to work out which toy has the largest head. Give him pieces of string to measure with. Mark the string with a different-coloured pen for each toy. Keep a record of the colours that you use.

● Make hand and feet prints of family members to compare and talk about sizes.

LEARNING OPPORTUNITY
● To talk about a theme, linking each statement to that main idea.

YOU WILL NEED
A table; shoebox; torch; string; paper clips; favourite soft toy; bar of chocolate; plastic mug; paper; pencil; plaster; small plastic bottle.

 STEPPING STONE
Link statements and stick to a main theme or intention.

EARLY LEARNING GOAL
Communication, language and literacy: Speak clearly and audibly with confidence and control.

Ready for adventure

Sharing the game
● Tell your child that you are both going to pretend that you are going on an adventure. Explain to her that you are going somewhere where there are no shops, a long way from any town.

● Show your child the shoebox. Say that you will not be able to carry much, and that you must choose to pack things in the box to take that will be really useful on your adventure.

● Lay out all the items on the table. Ask your child to choose something that she thinks will be really useful. When she has picked on, ask her to explain why her chosen item would be a good thing to take.

● Alternate with your child in choosing something to put in the shoebox, selecting approximately three items each.

Taking it further
● Ask your child if she can think of anything else that would fit in the shoebox that would be useful to take with you.
● Pretend to set out on your adventure. Take things from the box to use along the way, remembering why you packed them.
● Play 'Three reasons why'. Take it in turns to name an item and to give three reasons why it would not be a good idea to take the item with you.

LET'S PRETEND

LEARNING OPPORTUNITY
● To attempt to write simple words and to try more difficult words.

YOU WILL NEED
Two story-books, one featuring a cat and one featuring a dog; paper; pencils; cardboard boxes; small blanket or old pillowcases; string; ball of wool; small ball; paper plates; sticky tape.

 STEPPING STONE
Ascribe meanings to marks.

EARLY LEARNING GOAL
Communication, language and literacy: Use their phonic knowledge to write simple regular words and make phonetically plausible attempts at more complex words.

Home for a pet

Sharing the game
● Read the two stories to your child. Ask him which animal he would choose to have as a pet – a cat or a dog.
● Suggest that you pretend that he has got both pets and find out which would be harder to look after.
● Give your child the two boxes and ask him to make these into homes for the two pets. Suggest that the dog's home should be a kennel and the cat's home should be a basket.

Encourage your child to make the homes comfortable with the blankets or old pillowcases.
● Invite your child to label the homes. Help him to sound out the words 'dog' and 'cat', and to write a letter or mark for each sound. Let him tape the names to the boxes.
● Encourage your child to think about other things that the animals would need, for example, something to play with, a string lead for the dog and so on. Ask him to draw suitable food on the paper plates for each animal.

Taking it further
● Help your child to write a list of all the things that each animal needed. Use this to talk about the one that is harder to look after.
● Write lists of all the animals that you would both like to have as pets. Accept any attempt at writing that your child makes. Ask him to read his list to you.

CHAPTER 4

LIVELY TIMES

As children move through the Foundation Stage, between the ages of three to five, they begin to make connections between different ideas. They start to make the link between spoken and written language, realising that letters or numbers on a page can convey a message, in a similar way to the words that we say. The development of reading, writing and mathematical skills then takes place over a lengthy period. We can foster this development most effectively, if we recognise that young children learn best when they are using all of their senses, and if we provide opportunities that allow children a truly active role in learning.

ABSTRACT IDEAS

A great deal of the learning that children will be expected to undertake during their school years is rooted in abstract ideas. In reading and writing, letters are symbols for something else. The same is also true of numerals in mathematics. In science, children will need to understand that events can be linked by cause and effect.

We can help young children to make the leap to understanding these complex ideas by providing a transition stage. They will find it easier to begin to grasp some of these concepts if we introduce them in a more concrete form, appropriate for their learning style. Young children learn best when they can see ideas in action, and when they can touch, hear and see exactly what we are trying to teach them. They are not passive learners, waiting for us to provide them with information. They need to be physically involved in what we have to teach them.

How you can help
● Do not expect your child to sit still for long periods of time, engaged in quiet activities.

● Make ideas come alive for your child by linking them to familiar objects. For example, you could count out the knives and forks with him as you lay the table in order to reinforce the concept of numbers.
● Build words with magnetic or wooden letters so that your child can touch words and sounds.
● Help your child to grow and look after a plant to promote understanding of time concepts such as seasons.
● Lead your child into understanding ideas such as units of measurement by measuring objects in a variety of different ways, for example, measuring in shoe units, teddy units or hand spans.

words'. Try different categories, such as 'words that name our clothes' and 'words for feelings'.

● Look at non-fiction books with your child that contain labelled diagrams. Choose a subject that particularly interests her.

● As you read to your child, move your finger along the line of print, matching its movement with the words that you are reading.

● Clap out the beats in your child's name. Repeat with the names of other family members or friends.

● Play 'Robots'. Pretend to be a robot and say a word really slowly, broken up into its individual sounds. Ask your child to guess what you are saying.

the same first sound, and ask him to name them and tell you the sound that they all begin with.

● Play 'I spy' using the first sounds of objects rather than letter names.

● Put together a 'Sound presents' collection for each member of the family, based on items that begin with the same sound as each person's name. Enjoy the fact that some items may seem silly as presents.

● Look at picture alphabet books with your child to reinforce the idea that objects which begin with the same sound also begin with the same letter.

● Use wooden or plastic letters to familiarise your child with the abstract idea of a letter. It will help if he can feel the shape of the letters. Ask him to find things that begin with the sound that a certain letter makes, and display the objects and the letter together.

● Build a three-letter word and read it to your child. Encourage him to think of a rhyming word. Help him to change the first letter to make his new word.

CONNECTING THE SPOKEN AND THE WRITTEN WORD

Understanding that the abstract symbols which we call letters, represent the words that we speak, marks a major step in children's development. The written word is a prime method of communicating ideas in our education system, and in our world. Mastery of that written word opens the door for children to access all kinds of knowledge.

To begin to 'break the code' of written language, children first need to know that language is made up of units that we call words. Later, they realise that words can be broken down into syllables, and that these, in turn, are made up of individual sounds. This knowledge underlies both reading and spelling skills.

LETTER/SOUND LINK

One of the first steps on the road to literacy is the understanding of the link between individual letters and the sounds that they represent. To acquire this understanding, children need to be able to distinguish individual sounds in spoken words, and to learn that we use certain letters to represent these sounds. We focus, in the first place, on the initial sounds in words. If we are able to link the learning to concrete objects or to pictures, young children will find it much easier to master the necessary skills.

How you can help

● Play charades with your child, miming individual words. Cue her in, by explaining the type of word that you are miming. For example, you could say, 'Now I'm going to mime some action

How you can help

● Play games together that help your child to hear the first sounds in words. Make a collection of objects that begin with

LEARNING OPPORTUNITY
● To use talk to explain why certain choices have been made.

YOU WILL NEED
A range of clothes suitable for different seasons and different weather conditions.

 STEPPING STONE
Use talk to connect ideas.

EARLY LEARNING GOAL
Communication, language and literacy: Use talk to organise and clarify thinking.

Weather watch

Sharing the game
● Tell your child that you are going to play a dressing-up game. Lay out the clothes so that they are all easily visible and explain that different types of clothes are needed for this game.
● Choose an item of clothing, such as a thick jumper. Say, 'You might wear this because it would keep you warm on a really cold day. What else would

you put on if the weather was cold?'. Let your child choose another item of clothing and ask her why she has made that choice.
● Now say that you want her to pretend that the weather is very hot. Ask her to dress up, as quickly as she can, to go out in the hot weather. When she has made her choice of clothing, ask her to tell you why she chose each item.
● Take turns to say different types of weather for the other person to choose the clothes.
● Make the game more fun by challenging your child to put the new clothes on as quickly as she can!

Taking it further
● Rather than dressing for different weather conditions, ask your child to dress to go to different places or for different occasions. Always ask about the reasons for her choice afterwards.
● Provide a selection of objects linked with different weather, places or occasions on a nearby table, such as an umbrella, suntan lotion, sun-glasses and a Christmas cracker. Ask your child to choose an appropriate object to go with her chosen outfit.

LEARNING OPPORTUNITY
● To develop a sense of the beats (or syllables) in words.

YOU WILL NEED
A biscuit tin or saucepan; wooden spoons.

 STEPPING STONE
Enjoy rhyming and rhythmic activities.

 EARLY LEARNING GOAL
Communication, language and literacy: Hear and say initial and final sounds in words, and short vowel sounds within words.

Drummers

Sharing the game

● Invite your child to join in a drumming game with you. Explain to him that you are going to try to beat out the rhythm of some nursery rhymes together.

● Give your child a wooden spoon and encourage him to experiment with beating on a biscuit tin or upturned saucepan.

● Now tell your child that you are going to help him learn how to beat the drum in time with a rhyme. Start with 'Mary Had a Little Lamb' (Traditional) which has a very regular, simple beat. Say the rhyme, a line at a time, beating on the 'drum' in time with the

syllables of the words. Ask your child to repeat each line after you, beating the rhythm just like you have done. If he is having difficulty fitting the beat to the words, hold his hand to help him.

● Try the rhyme again, this time beating it out together, rather than providing a model for him to copy.

Taking it further

● Use different rhymes, gradually increasing the difficulty of the rhythm. A good progression would be 'Mary, Mary, Quite Contrary', 'Jack and Jill', 'I Had a Little Nut Tree' and 'Tom, Tom, the Piper's Son' (all Traditional).

● Choose some everyday instructions that have a different number of beats, such as 'Time for tea', 'Time to get bathed' and 'Time to go to bed'. Practise beating them out with your child, then see if he can guess your message from just listening to the beats. Let him try sending you one of these messages for you to guess, too.

Up, over and under

LIVELY TIMES

LEARNING OPPORTUNITY
● To learn the language of position and direction.

YOU WILL NEED
Two soft toys.

Sharing the game
● Invite your child to join you in taking the soft toys for a walk around the room. Explain to her that you are going to try to help your toy to move around as many things in the room in as many different ways as possible.

● Lead your toy around the room, suggesting to your child that she follow with her toy.
● As you move, provide a commentary, saying, for example, 'I'm going to take Teddy forwards towards the chair. Then he's going to go under the chair.' Ask your child, at each step, to tell you where her toy is going.
● Use as many different position and direction words as you can, taking the toy 'around the lamp', 'over the sofa', 'through the door' and so on. Help the toy to move forwards and backwards, to the left, to the right and around objects.
● Let your child plan, and talk you through, the next route. Make your toy follow the route that her toy takes.

Taking it further
● Hide a small object in the room and give your child instructions for a route to find it.
● Set up an obstacle course with a chair, mat, cardboard box (opened up similar to a tunnel) and a stick with the ends resting on two boxes. Let your child explore different ways of moving around the course, telling you whether she is going to go over or under the stick, through or around the box and so on.

STEPPING STONE Build up vocabulary that reflects the breadth of their experiences.

EARLY LEARNING GOAL Communication, language and literacy: Extend their vocabulary, exploring the meanings and sounds of new words.

● ●

LEARNING OPPORTUNITY
● To understand the idea of a word and to tell a simple story.

YOU WILL NEED
Just you and your child.

My cat, Claws

Sharing the game

● Explain to your child that you are going to tell him a story, but you are going to leave out some of the words. Say that you will use actions to help him to guess the missing words. Tell him that the story is about a cat, who likes to have night-time adventures.

● Begin the story by saying, 'When everyone is asleep each night, my cat Claws slips ____ the cat flap, out into the garden'. Instead of using the word 'through', make a circle with the thumb and forefinger of one hand and push the forefinger of the other hand through it. Ask your child to guess the missing word.

● Continue the story. Make Claws creep down (make a down action with your hand) the garden path, climb up (make an up action with your hand) a tree and leap on to (bring one palm down on to the other) the roof of the shed. Make Claws go over, under and around objects, before he slips back (point to your back) home, just as everyone is waking up. Each time that you omit and mime a word, encourage your child to suggest what the missing word is.

● Now invite your child to make up his version of the story, while you guess the words that he is miming.

Taking it further

● Tell the story again, or a different story, missing out action words such as walk, jump, run, leap and so on, and mime these instead.

● Take turns to make up a sentence each, and guess each other's mimed action words.

 STEPPING STONE
Understand the concept of a word.

EARLY LEARNING GOAL
Communication, language and literacy: Retell narratives in the correct sequence, drawing on language patterns of stories.

LEARNING OPPORTUNITY
● To learn that certain items belong together in categories, and that there are special names for these categories.

YOU WILL NEED
A ride-on toy; collection of home-made cards with pictures of different foods and drinks, cut from magazines, stuck on to each card. (Make sure that you have several cards for each category, such as fruit, vegetables, meat and so on.)

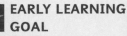 **STEPPING STONE**
Extend vocabulary, especially by grouping and naming.

EARLY LEARNING GOAL
Communication, language and literacy: Extend their vocabulary, exploring the meanings and sounds of new words.

Home delivery

Sharing the game
● Invite your child to play a game with you, pretending that you are a shopkeeper and that she is the delivery person, who brings you all the things that you need for your shop.
● Lay out the food cards in random order. As you do so, say, for example, 'Here's some more fruit – apples this time'. When all the cards are laid out, tell your child that she must wait for

your order, and then deliver it to you in her lorry. Have the ride-on toy ready for her to use.
● Go to the other side of the room and pretend to telephone your child. Say that you would like to place an order for as many different kinds of vegetables as she has. Wait for your child to deliver the cards to you, then tell her that you are going to check your order to make sure that she has only brought you the vegetables that you asked for.
● Continue playing the game with your child, ordering different categories of food, such as fruit and meat.

Taking it further
● Use the game to develop your child's understanding of categories beyond the basic meat, fruit and vegetable categories. Introduce the idea of cereals, dairy food, bakery items and so on.
● Use paper plates and ask your child to create a meal with the cards by choosing items from the different categories that you name.

LEARNING OPPORTUNITY
● To respond appropriately to a simple instruction and to learn a variety of movement words.

YOU WILL NEED
Just you and your child.

STEPPING STONE
Respond to simple instructions.

EARLY LEARNING GOAL
Communication, language and literacy: Sustain attentive listening, responding to what they have heard by relevant actions.

How many ways?

Sharing the game

● Invite your child to play a game to show you just how carefully he can listen, and to show you how many different ways he can move.

● Explain that you are going to ask him a question, and then tell him to cross the room in a particular way. Say that you want him to show you that he can do it.

● Say, 'How many ways can you cross the room? I'd like you to try to slither like a snake'. Then as your child carries out the instruction, encourage him to tell you what he is doing, using the appropriate movement word.

● Continue to give him instructions for a variety of movements. Ask him to hop like a kangaroo, to stamp like a rhino, to waddle like a goose, to skip like a lamb, and so on.

● Encourage your child to challenge you to cross the room in different ways, to practise the different words that he has learned.

Taking it further

● Set a short time span, such as fifteen minutes. Tell your child that any time you clap your hands during that time, he should stop what he is doing and listen very carefully. You will whisper an instruction, and he must carry it out.

● Make your instructions funny, such as telling him to put a pair of shorts on his head, or rewarding, such as, 'Come and have a hug'. Give your child lots of praise for listening carefully and doing what he was told.

● Let him give you instructions, in the same way.

LEARNING OPPORTUNITY
● To hear and say the first sound in the child's name and to know which letter writes that sound.

YOU WILL NEED
A cardboard box; scissors; glue; old magazines.

 STEPPING STONE
Hear and say the initial sound in words and know which letters represent some of the sounds.

EARLY LEARNING GOAL
Communication, language and literacy: Hear and say initial sounds in words.

My special box

Sharing the game
● Suggest to your child that she might like to make a special box to keep things in, with her own name letter on it, to show that it belongs to her.
● Ask her to say her name and then to tell you the very first sound that she hears in her name. Suggest that you both look through the old magazines for pictures of things that begin with the same sound. When you find appropriate pictures, cut them out and glue them on to the outside of the box.

● Say that now you are going to look for the letter that writes the first sound in her name. Find a large version of that capital letter in a magazine. Let her cut it out, and glue it on to the box. If your child's name begins with a 'th', 'sh' or 'ch' sound, find the two letters that write the sound. Explain that the first sound in her name needs two letters to write it.
● Find as many versions of your child's initial letter as you can and let her decorate her special box with them.

Taking it further
● Glue an envelope to the top of a shoebox. Inside the box, place a few items that begin with the same sound. Slip a card into the envelope with the appropriate letter written on it. Give the 'surprise box' to your child and invite her to look at it. Help her to discover the common initial sound of the objects inside, then take out the card for her to see how that sound is written.

LEARNING OPPORTUNITY
● To develop the fine motor skills which are needed to be able to write effectively.

YOU WILL NEED
Empty cereal boxes; pencil; scissors; ruler.

 STEPPING STONE
Manipulate objects with increasing control.

EARLY LEARNING GOAL
Communication, language and literacy: Use a pencil and hold it effectively to form recognisable letters.

As a rule

Sharing the game
● Show your child the ruler, and ask if he knows what it is used for. Talk about how it helps you to measure things. Ask your child if he would like to help you to make a special kind of ruler to measure some things.
● Open out the cereal box and ask your child to place one of his shoes on the back of the card. Tell him to draw around the shoe, using the pencil. Now ask him to cut out the shoe 'ruler' that he has drawn. Help, if necessary. Make four or five shoe measures in this way.
● Explain that he is going to check 'how many shoes long' the table is. Show him how to place the heel end of one of his measures at the edge of the table, and to place the others in a row, with no gaps in between. When he runs out of measures, show him how to use a finger to mark where the toe end of the last measure comes to, while he moves another measure along. Explain to your child that it is important not to move the finger until the next measure is in position. Help him to keep count of the number of shoes needed to reach along the length of the table.
● Encourage him to measure a variety of different objects, or the size of rooms.

Taking it further
● Make a chart for your child to record the measurements that he has just taken. Use tally marks, or numbers, according to his current stage of development.
● Make 'shoe measures' from other family members.

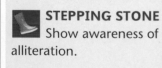

LEARNING OPPORTUNITY
● To hear accurately the first sounds in words.

YOU WILL NEED
Just you and your child.

STEPPING STONE
Show awareness of alliteration.

EARLY LEARNING GOAL
Communication, language and literacy: Hear and say initial sounds in words.

Fingers, feet

Sharing the game
● Stand facing your child, making sure that there is enough space around you.
● Explain that you are going to play a game to see who can be quickest to point to different parts of the body. Tell her that you will name a part of her body and that she must point to it as fast as she can. Say, 'Nose', emphasising the 'n' sound at the beginning, and place your forefinger on your nose to show what you want her to do.
● Say that you are going to name another part of the body that starts with the same sound as nose. Tell her that she must point to that part as quickly as she can, to see if she can beat you.
● Say, 'Neck', extending the first sound to draw attention to it. Move your finger to your neck.
● Repeat this using different parts of the body from the list below. Remember that it is the sound, not the spelling, that is important.
  – fingers, feet, forehead
  – neck, knee, nose, knuckle, nail
  – teeth, toes, tongue
  – head, hands, heels, hip, hair
  – back, bottom
  – shin, shoulder
  – chin, cheek
  – thigh, thumb.

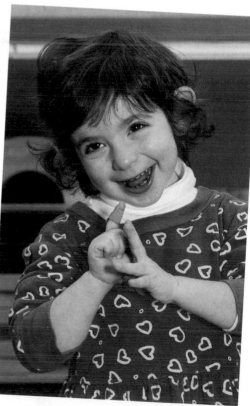

Taking it further
● Give the first word only and let your child guess what the second one is going to be, using the clue of the first sound.
● Name three parts of the body, two of which begin with the same sound. Invite your child to point to the part of the body that begins with the sound that is different from the other two.

LEARNING OPPORTUNITY
● To learn the sounds and the names of the letters of the alphabet.

YOU WILL NEED
Twenty-six pegs; sticky labels; pen; length of strong string; 26 small items or pictures, each beginning with a different letter of the alphabet (for the vowels, use things that begin with the vowel sounds, as in 'apple', 'elephant', 'igloo', 'orange' and 'umbrella'; for the letter 'x', use a picture of a fox or a small box).

 STEPPING STONE Hear and say the initial sound in words and know which letters represent some of the sounds.

 EARLY LEARNING GOAL Communication, language and literacy: Link sounds to letters, naming and sounding the letters of the alphabet.

A to z

Sharing the game
● Set up a line by tying the string between two chairs, for example.
● Label each peg with a lower-case letter of the alphabet, using the sticky labels. Place the pegs in alphabetical order along the line.
● Ask your child to help you find the correct object to go with each letter. Show the object beginning with 'a' and ask for its name. Ask for the sound at the beginning of the word. Clip it to the 'a' peg, saying, 'The letter "a" writes the sound "a"'. Encourage your child to repeat, 'Apple, "a" (sound), "a" (name)'.

● Work though the alphabet, letting your child peg up each item, saying the picture, the sound and then the letter name. With 'fox' or 'box', ask your child for the last sound.

Taking it further
● When your child knows the alphabet order, put the pegs on the line in random order, and ask him to sort them into the correct sequence.
● Use three pegs to peg up simple words. Encourage your child to say the sounds as you add each peg, then blend them together into a word. Use only words with a clear link between individual letters and sounds, such as cat, hat, dog, log and so on.

LEARNING OPPORTUNITY
● To name the letters of the alphabet and to link these names with the sounds the letters make.

YOU WILL NEED
A copy of the instructions for the 'Active alphabet' on page 125.

STEPPING STONE
Hear and say the initial sound in words and know which letters represent some of the sounds.

EARLY LEARNING GOAL
Communication, language and literacy: Link sounds to letters, naming and sounding the letters of the alphabet.

Alphabet activities

Sharing the game
● Explain to your child that you are going to play an exercise game, using the letters of the alphabet. Tell her that you will say the name of each letter in turn. Say that you will give the sound of the letter after its name and say a word with that sound in it. Ask her to listen to the word and to watch you carefully as you show her exactly what she needs to do.
● Make sure that you have plenty of space around you

before you begin the game. Give the name of the letter 'a', then say its sound (as in 'apple'). Say the word 'attention', emphasising an 'a' sound at the beginning. As you say the word, stand up very straight, with your arms by your side. Give your child the instructions to do the same.
● Continue in this way, until you have worked through the alphabet. With a very young child, you may wish to break the alphabet up into sections, adding a further section as your child becomes familiar with the previous ones. There are natural rest points built into the activity sequence, to enable you to do this or simply to take a rest.

Taking it further
● Choose some letters of the alphabet to see if you and your child can think of alternative activities to perform, for example, 'b' for 'balance' (stand on one leg), 'r' for 'ride' (ride your bike) and so on.

LEARNING OPPORTUNITY
● To recognise the names of the letters of the alphabet, and to be able to give the sounds of those letters.

YOU WILL NEED
Card (the back of card from cereal packets is useful, but stronger card will allow for reuse many times); thick marker pen; blanket or rug.

STEPPING STONE
Hear and say the initial sound in words and know which letters represent some of the sounds.

EARLY LEARNING GOAL
Communication, language and literacy: Link sounds to letters, naming and sounding the letters of the alphabet.

Cross the river

Sharing the game

● Cut out 26 large pieces of card into stepping-stone shapes (they need not be exactly the same shape). Write one letter of the alphabet on each 'stone' in bold lower case.

● Show the cards to your child, explaining that they are stepping-stones to help him cross the river safely. If you think that your child would enjoy the added fun, mention that the river is full of crocodiles.

● Lay the rug out on the floor and scatter about eight cards on to it. Say that you can see where the crocodiles are, and that the safe way across the river is... (name three letters here). Then repeat the first letter, telling your child to step on to that card. Ask him to tell you the sound that the letter makes (to keep the crocodiles away). Repeat this with the second and third letters.

● Try different routes across the river until your child is thoroughly used to all the letters. Then change the selection. Make sure that you teach the 'x' sound, as in 'box'.

Taking it further

● Give routes across the river that spell out simple three-letter words. When your child has crossed once, encourage him to take the same route again, crossing quickly and sounding each letter in quick sequence. Ask him to blend all the sounds together into a word.

LIVELY TIMES

Skittles

LIVELY TIMES

LEARNING OPPORTUNITY
● To be able to give the sound made by a letter of the alphabet, and to think of a word beginning with that sound.

YOU WILL NEED
Empty plastic drinks bottles; paper; felt-tipped pen; small ball.

STEPPING STONE
Hear and say the initial sound in words and know which letters represent some of the sounds.

EARLY LEARNING GOAL
Communication, language and literacy: Link sounds to letters, naming and sounding the letters of the alphabet.

Sharing the game
● Starting with just three or four bottles, write a letter for each bottle on a piece of paper and tape it to the bottle. Invite your child to play a game of skittles with you.
● Explain that, in this game, the idea is not just to knock down the skittles. Tell your child that, when she knocks over a bottle, she must look at the letter on it, tell you the sound the letter makes, and then tell you a word beginning with that sound. She must do this for each bottle as she knocks it over.

● Take it in turns to aim for the skittles and to think of words. Explain that a word cannot be used more than once. Help your child by giving clues for a word, if she is having difficulty thinking of one. Make sure that you accept any word that begins with the correct sound, even if the spelling would not use that letter, for example, knee for the 'n' sound.
● As your child becomes used to the game, add a few more skittles, so that more might be knocked over, challenging her to think of more words.

Taking it further
● Decide on different categories of words, such as animals, or foods, and try to come up with words in that category beginning with the target sound.
● Help your child to hunt through newspaper headlines, looking for words beginning with given letters. Read them out.

LEARNING OPPORTUNITY
● To begin to recognise and read some simple words.

YOU WILL NEED
Ten pieces of card, approximately the size of playing cards; pen.

 STEPPING STONE
Begin to recognise some familiar words.

 EARLY LEARNING GOAL
Communication, language and literacy: Read a range of familiar and common words.

Hop it

Sharing the game
● Write the words 'run', 'skip', 'hop', 'jump' and 'sit' clearly on five of the cards. Repeat the words on the other cards, adding a pin-man drawing beside the word to illustrate the action.
● Invite your child to try to win cards by carrying out the action written on the card you show him.
● Show your child each of the illustrated cards in turn. Explain that the picture helps him to understand what the word says. Point to the word

and read it. Ask your child to repeat the word.
● Shuffle the cards. Ask your child to read the first word to you, and then to do what it says. If he gets the word right, and carries out the action, he wins the card. If he is incorrect, place the card back in the pack and try another.
● When your child is used to the game, explain that you are going to try it without the pictures. Change the cards to the five with the words only.

Taking it further
● Lay out a trail of the cards, leaving spaces between them. Starting at the first card, your child must read the word, and perform that action, as he moves towards the next card. He then reads that card and changes the action to move to the third. If the card says 'sit', he must move along on his bottom. Change the order of the cards, and time him to see if he can reach the end quicker the second time.
● Add new action words to the pack. Choose simple words, such as 'sing', 'hum', 'walk' and so on.

CHAPTER 5

QUIET TIMES

For young children to master reading and writing, many underlying skills need to be in place. To learn our letter system, for example, children must be able to see similarities and note small differences. Those who have had practice with other motor skills, and are well co-ordinated, will acquire the complex skills of writing more easily. Children will enjoy books more if they already have a sense of how stories are put together and how books work. They will be more motivated to learn to read if they understand that books can provide them with interesting and useful information.

LOOKING AT DETAIL

Many of the 26 letters in the English alphabet, have very similar features. The addition of one small extra mark can change one letter into another. Pairs of words may also have features in common. The words 'there' and 'three', for example, share the same letters, in a different order. The words 'fog' and 'frog' differ by only one letter. In order to learn to read proficiently, children must be able to distinguish the smallest differences between letters and words. They need to be able to look in detail, in order to process words accurately.

How you can help

● As you read to your child, look at the illustrations together and encourage your child to talk to you about the pictures.

● Help your child to be alert to the world around her. Point out small details to her as you carry out everyday activities together.

● Look out for books that offer practice in 'spot the difference' activities.

● Draw a small ladybird on a piece of card. Cut it out and 'hide' it on a picture with lots of detail. Ask your child to find it for you. Wrapping paper with detailed scenes can be ideal for this type of activity.

● Choose a piece of wrapping paper, or a page in a children's book, showing simple, clean-line objects. Trace different objects, filling in the outline to make a silhouette picture. Cut it out.

Ask your child to place the silhouette on top of the appropriate item on the page or paper.

UNDERSTANDING HOW BOOKS WORK

We sometimes assume that young children know automatically how books work. Yet, even seeing us flick through a book, or magazine, from back to front, can give misleading signals about the most basic message: that we start a book from the front and work through to the back. Children need to understand, too, how print is laid out on the page, that we begin reading at the top and work left to right down to the bottom of a page. Beyond this, they need to understand how stories are structured, and that print can convey other factual information, as well as story lines.

How you can help
● Read to your child regularly. Talk about the characters or parts of the book that you particularly like, and encourage your child to do the same.
● Look at the cover of a book and show your child how it gives us information about the writer and, on the back cover, an idea of what the book is about.
● Pause as you read the story. Discuss with your child what he thinks might happen next.
● Hold your child's hand and help him to track the words as you read them.
● Make up stories together. Use amusing family events as the basis of a book. Tell the story of the day the family hamster escaped. Write down your child's words and let him illustrate the book.
● Share non-fiction books, as well as fiction. Pick up on your child's interests, whether it be dinosaurs or wildlife, and show him how books can tell him more about the subject.

AWARENESS OF RHYME
Children would take a very long time to learn to read and write if they had to memorise every single word separately. An awareness that words which share the same sound, often share a common spelling, eases the task. Young children first become aware of this through rhyme. They begin to notice that some words have the same ending sounds. We know that young children who have a good awareness of rhyme, and who then make the link between rhymes in words and the same letter pattern in those words, are at an advantage when reading and spelling.

How you can help
● Enjoy reading nursery rhymes and poems to your child.
● When you are reading rhymes, omit the rhyming word. Wait for your child to supply it. Play a game, in which she substitutes a different rhyming word to make a silly rhyme.
● Play 'I hear' instead of 'I spy'. Say, 'I hear with my little ear, something that rhymes with…'. Say a word, and ask your child for a rhyming word.
● Play 'Odd word out'. Say three words, two of which rhyme. Ask your child to name the word that doesn't rhyme. Don't always give the non-rhyming word in the same position. If your child is beginning to read simple three-letter words, write the three words down, and ask her to pick the odd word out.

MANIPULATING A PENCIL
Being able to manipulate a pencil efficiently for writing requires young children to develop good fine motor skills. Before they can do this, they need to have acquired other, larger motor skills. They need good balance to be able to sit appropriately. They must be able to separate the movements of the two hands (in writing one hand anchors the paper, while the other writes). They must have good hand–eye co-ordination. These skills are often perfected in activities that appear to have little to do with writing, such as catching a ball.

It is important to realise that young children cannot perfect the tiny movements needed for writing if they have not mastered the underlying bigger movements first.

How you can help
● Provide plenty of opportunities for activities, such as ball games, that promote hand–eye co-ordination.
● Encourage activities that help to develop large motor movements (swimming is useful) and balance, making sure that these are safely supervised.
● Let your child help with cooking activities. Rolling pastry, cutting shapes, mixing and kneading, all help to develop the hand and finger strength and flexibility needed for writing.
● Remember that practice with tools such as scissors will help to prepare your child for the precision movements that she will need for writing.

LEARNING OPPORTUNITY
● To begin to understand how to tell a story.

YOU WILL NEED
Pictures from magazines (or postcards) with plenty of detail.

 STEPPING STONE
Suggest how the story might end.

 EARLY LEARNING GOAL
Communication, language and literacy: Show an understanding of the elements of stories, such as sequence of events and openings.

Pick a picture

Sharing the game
● Invite your child to join you for a storytelling game.
● Show him one of your chosen pictures. Explain that you are going to start a sentence about the picture. Say that you will begin the sentence, but that you would like him to finish it for you.
● Demonstrate exactly what you mean. If, for example, you are using

an advertisement picture of a kitchen, with a small girl eating breakfast, you might say, 'Far away, in a house just like ours, there once lived... Now, I want you to finish the sentence off, by telling me who lived in the house far away'.

● When you have worked through a number of pictures, suggest that you start again, but this time, that you try to make up a longer story, by saying one sentence each. Build it up in this way, until you are taking it in turns to make up a short story. When you give your opening sentence, try to use the sort of opening phrases that your child might find in story-books.

Taking it further
● Choose two pictures which have some possible link. Start a sentence, leaving it unfinished and ending with a word such as 'but' or 'when'. Show your child the second picture and ask him to finish the sentence by saying something about this picture.
● Write down some of the stories that you have made up together. Put them in a ring binder with the relevant pictures, and label it on the front with your child's name. Make time to read '(*your child's name*)'s stories' together.

LEARNING OPPORTUNITY
● To develop the skill of asking questions, and conversing with others.

YOU WILL NEED
A piece of paper; pencil.

 STEPPING STONE
Ask simple questions, often in the form of 'where' or 'what'.

EARLY LEARNING GOAL
Communication, language and literacy: Interact with others, taking turns in conversation.

No no, no yes

Sharing the game
● Explain to your child that you are going to play a question-and-answer game. Tell her that you are going to take turns to ask each other any question you like. The other person must answer honestly, but cannot use the words 'yes' or 'no'.

● Show your child how to play the game. Say, 'You could ask me the question, "Do you like chocolate?". I can't say, "Yes", so I would have to say, for example, "I do like chocolate"'. Take it in turns to ask and answer questions. Ask about the colour of eyes

and hair, where your child lives, and so on, phrasing the question so that she must avoid using the words 'yes' and 'no'. Ask, for example, 'Do you live in America?'. Help your child to formulate questions to ask you, if necessary.

● If you manage to avoid the forbidden words, you score a point. Keep a record, on a piece of paper, of points won. Make an occasional error yourself, to boost your child's confidence.

Taking it further
● Suggest a series of interesting 'people'. Discuss with your child what one question she would like to ask that person, if she could meet him or her. Choose a variety of different people, such as the first man on the moon, a character from her favourite book, a cartoon character and the Queen.

LEARNING OPPORTUNITY
● To provide explanations for a line of thinking.

YOU WILL NEED
An A4 envelope; selection of pictures of single objects, cut from catalogues or magazines.

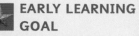 **STEPPING STONE** Question why things happen, and give explanations.

 **EARLY LEARNING GOAL**
Communication, language and literacy: Enjoy listening to and using spoken language, and readily turn to it in their play and learning.

What could it be?

Sharing the game
● Choose a selection of pictures of objects with which your child is familiar. Slip one of the pictures into the envelope, top of the picture first, so that as you pull it out, the bottom will be revealed first. Ask your child if he would like to play a guessing game with you.
● Explain that you have a picture in the envelope of something he knows. Tell him that you will show him a little bit of the picture, and he has to guess what it is.
● Slip the picture just a little way out of the envelope to reveal the bottom. Ask your child what he sees. If, for example, his answer is 'Four paws', ask if he thinks that the picture could be a car, or a horse. As he gives his reply, encourage him to explain why the picture could or could not be the item under discussion.
● Slip the picture a little further out of the envelope and invite your child to guess again, explaining his guess, until he names the item correctly.
● Change the picture.

Taking it further
● Make some simple line drawings of objects and use these in the game instead of magazine pictures.
● After trying the game with line drawings, try it again with letters. Write them in bold lower case on pieces of paper, and help your child with questions such as, 'Which letters have a curly tail like this?'.

LEARNING OPPORTUNITY
● To sort things in a variety of ways, according to different descriptive characteristics.

YOU WILL NEED
A collection of animal pictures cut from magazines.

 STEPPING STONE
Use talk to connect ideas.

EARLY LEARNING GOAL
Communication, language and literacy: Use talk to organise ideas.

Different sorts

Sharing the game
● Spread the pictures out on the table and ask your child to help you sort them into groups. Explain that you are going to try to find out how many different ways the pictures can be sorted.
● Start by suggesting that you sort the animals into those that are wild, those that live on farms and those that could be pets. Encourage your child to talk about her choices as she makes them. Talk about which group is the largest. Ask her if she can think of any other animals that could belong to any of the groups.

● Jumble up the pictures again and suggest that, now, you try to sort the pictures into animals with long tails, those with short tails and those with no tails. Talk about choices as you sort the pictures.
● Try other sorting categories, for example, animals with fur and animals with feathers; four-legged and two-legged animals; animals with patterns and those without, and so on. Each time, encourage your child to think of any other animals that could be added to the groups. Stop when your child shows signs of tiring.

Taking it further
● Keep lists of the groups of animals. When you stop the sorting game, look at the lists and choose one animal, for example, a horse. Say to your child, 'I can see the horse in lots of groups. The horse is a four-legged animal, with a long tail and no pattern that can be a pet'. Encourage your child to choose another animal and tell you all she can about it.

QUIET TIMES

LEARNING OPPORTUNITY
● To look at the detail of pictures and to talk through small differences.

YOU WILL NEED
Pairs of the same picture, either taken from wrapping paper with repeat pictures or simple line drawings, made using carbon paper to produce the second picture; coloured pens.

STEPPING STONE
Talk activities through, reflecting on what they are doing.

EARLY LEARNING GOAL
Communication, language and literacy: Use talk to clarify thinking.

What's the difference?

Sharing the game
● Choose a pair of pictures and invite your child to look at them with you. Ask him to tell you whether the pictures look the same. Look together at the detail of the picture. Ask questions about the colours of, for example, a creature, or the number of spots it has.
● When you have ascertained that the pictures are the same, say that you are going to change one of the pictures to make it different. Do this away from your child. Put an extra button on clothing, colour something differently, and so on.
● Show your child the pictures again and ask him to see if he can notice anything that is different in one of them.
● Once your child has got the idea of the game, prepare other pairs of pictures in advance and encourage him to spot the differences straight away.

Taking it further
● Use three pictures and alter only one. Ask your child to find the odd picture out.
● Prepare a number of identical pairs of pictures and stick them to the same size squares of card. Turn all the pictures over on the table and play 'Pairs', taking it in turn to turn over two cards to see if they match. If the cards are a pair, the player takes those cards. If not, they are turned back over. The winner is the player with the most pairs.

LEARNING OPPORTUNITY
● To make up a story, based on everyday experience.

YOU WILL NEED
Paper; staple or wool; pencils; pen; colouring pens.

Tell me a story

Sharing the game

● Suggest to your child that she might like to make a book with you about a day in her life. Fold a few sheets of paper. Staple them together or tie some wool around the folds to hold them together in a book format. Make a book of only four or six pages, to begin with.

● Show your child the front page and say, 'Let's put the title on here. I'll write, "Sarah's day, by Sarah"'. Ask if she would like to draw a picture of herself on the book cover.

● Talk through the sort of things that your child does each day. Encourage her to draw colourful pictures of herself on each page of the book. Ask her to tell you something about what she is doing in the pictures. Use one sentence per page, writing down exactly what she says to you.

● Continue until the book is filled, or until your child says that the book is finished.

Taking it further

● Choose other familiar topics as the subject of home-made books. If your child has a pet, make this the focus, or encourage your child to make up a book about the family.

● Use copies of family photos as the illustrations for a book. An extra set of photos from a holiday can form the focus for your child to make up her own story of that holiday.

● Encourage her to begin trying to write some of the words herself, starting with her name, when it appears in the story.

 STEPPING STONE
Describe main story settings, events and principal characters.

EARLY LEARNING GOAL
Communication, language and literacy: Listen with enjoyment, and respond to stories and make up their own stories.

QUIET TIMES

LEARNING OPPORTUNITY
● To practise pre-writing movements and control of a pencil.

YOU WILL NEED
Paper; pencils; colouring pencils.

 STEPPING STONE
Manipulate objects with increasing control.

EARLY LEARNING GOAL
Communication, language and literacy: Use a pencil and hold it effectively.

Draw a clown

Sharing the game
● Ask your child if he would like you to show him how to draw a clown. Explain that you will tell him what to do, one bit at a time.
● Sit beside your child and draw the clown, stage by stage, so that he can see exactly what to do. Encourage him to follow your lead. Give these instructions (the stages are illustrated on page 127):

1 Draw a circle like this.
2 Draw two small circles for eyes.
3 Now add a bigger circle for the clown's nose.
4 Draw these two lines to make a hat.
5 Now draw a circle on top of the hat.
6 Draw a wavy line to make a frill around the clown's neck.
7 Draw zigzag lines to make hair.
8 Put a big smile on your clown.

● As your child draws, try to ensure that he is holding the pencil with the correct grip. The pencil should be held between the thumb and forefinger, with the middle finger acting as a rest. If this is difficult for your child, you can try wrapping a wide elastic band around the pencil to make it easier to grip.
● Encourage him to colour in the clown that he has drawn.

Taking it further
● Add a body to the clown, and ask your child to draw zigzag and wavy-lined patterns on the clown's clothes.
● Try using books of simple mazes to provide practice in manipulating a pencil.
● Provide plenty of paper and a variety of writing implements for your child to experiment with writing.

Guess the picture!

Sharing the game

● Invite your child to play a drawing game. Draw a circle on a piece of paper and show it to your child. Explain that you are going to change the circle into a picture.

● Draw two small circles inside the first one, in the position of eyes. Talk as you draw. Say to your child, 'Look, I'm putting two circles inside of the big one. Have you any idea what they might be?'.

● Draw two lines down from the bottom of the circle to make a neck, again describing what you are doing and asking if your child can guess what the picture is. Then draw snaky lines out from the top and sides of the circle, to make some hair.

● Next add two small dots for a nose, and finally add a curved line for a mouth, each time talking through what you are doing. If your child guesses the picture before completion, invite her to finish the picture.

● Now give your child a turn at drawing a picture. Give her a circle to start with and ask her to talk to you about what she is doing, as she makes it into a picture.

● Try a variety of different shapes as starting-points.

● If your child has difficulty in thinking what to do, present a number of options, for example, circles can be the centres of flowers, wheels or portholes on a ship; squares might be houses, robots or elephants' bodies; and so on.

Taking it further

● Use the illustrations on page 126 as a guide to draw some simple pictures for your child. Let her complete your dotted-line drawings. Encourage her to talk about the shapes that she can see and that she is drawing as she goes over the lines to finish each picture.

 STEPPING STONE Manipulate objects with increasing control.

EARLY LEARNING GOAL
Communication, language and literacy: Use a pencil and hold it effectively.

LEARNING OPPORTUNITY
● To recognise words as units in a sentence.

YOU WILL NEED
A sheet of A4 paper; pencil; six counters.

STEPPING STONE
Begin to break the flow of speech into words.

EARLY LEARNING GOAL
Communication, language and literacy: Write their own names and other things such as labels and captions and begin to form simple sentences.

How many words?

Sharing the game

● Place the piece of paper sideways and draw a rectangle in the middle, stretching right across the paper. Draw five lines to divide the rectangle into six boxes across the page.

● Invite your child to play a word game with you. Show him the boxes, and ask him to put a coloured counter beneath each one.

● Explain that you are going to say a sentence to him, and that you want him to repeat the sentence after you. Tell him that, as he says the sentence, he should push one counter into a box for each word he says. Make sure that he understands that he should begin with the left-hand box and work across to the right of the page.

● Begin with a simple sentence of three words, for example, 'It is sunny'. Check that your child pushes one counter into a box for each word he repeats. Then try a four-word sentence.

● If you are happy that your child has understood the idea, begin to use sentences of varying length, up to six words. Use commands such as, 'Sit down!' or statements such as, 'Mummy laughs', for two-word sentences.

Taking it further

● Build up a sentence by one person giving a word, and then taking it in turns to add words. The person who says the word that completes a sentence wins a point.

● Count the number of words on the front covers of books.

● Count how many words your child can think of to describe himself.

LEARNING OPPORTUNITY
● To learn that marks can convey a message.

YOU WILL NEED
Paper; coloured pencils; card; three different-coloured buttons or counters.

 STEPPING STONE
Ascribe meanings to marks.

EARLY LEARNING GOAL
Communication, language and literacy: Attempt writing for different purposes.

First to the finish

Sharing the game

● Draw a grid six squares by six on the paper. At the top left corner, just outside of the grid, draw a red arrow pointing right. At the top right corner, draw a green arrow pointing down. At the bottom right corner, draw a black arrow pointing left. At the bottom left corner, draw a blue arrow pointing up.

● Cut out 12 small cards. Draw each arrow, as described above, on three cards, so that all 12 cards show an arrow. Shuffle, and place face-down on the table.

● Cut 12 more small cards and write each of the numerals 1 to 6 on two cards. Shuffle and place face-down on the table.

● Invite your child to play the game with you. Ask her to place one counter anywhere on the grid, except the bottom left square. Explain that, in the game, you must both try to reach this counter with your own. Place your two playing counters in the bottom left square to begin.

● Ask your child to pick up an arrow card and a number card. Show her that this tells her in which direction, and how many squares to move. Now take it in turns to choose cards and move counters. After each go, place the used cards back at the bottom of the appropriate pile. The first player to land on the same square as the target counter, wins the game.

Taking it further

● Enlarge the grid to a ten-by-ten square and add more number cards to the pile.
● Omit the arrows and make word cards with 'up', 'down', 'right' and 'left' written on them.

QUIET TIMES

LEARNING OPPORTUNITY
● To learn the shape of letters and how to form them.

YOU WILL NEED
A baking tray; large bag of salt.

STEPPING STONE
Begin to form recognisable letters.

EARLY LEARNING GOAL
Communication, language and literacy: Use a pencil and hold it effectively to form recognisable letters.

Now you see it...

Sharing the game
● Cover the base of the baking tray with salt. Tell your child that you are going to play a game with letters.
● Ask your child to name something that he can see in the room. Then, ask what sound he hears at the beginning of that word. Say, 'I'm going to write the letter that writes that sound'. Draw the letter in the salt, using your forefinger. Use lower case, not capital letters. Describe the movements you are making, as you write. For example, when writing the letter 'h', say, 'I go down, back up, and over in a hump'.
● Ask your child to trace around the letter shape you have made, with his forefinger. Then shake the tray and say, 'Would you like to try to write that letter yourself now?'. Describe the movements, as you did before, to help him. When he has finished, name the item he chose, say the first sound, then say the letter name, holding his hand to trace around his letter again.
● Let him choose further things that he can see, and practise other letter shapes. Try to avoid items that do not start with a single letter sound, such as chairs. Just suggest that you will come back to that one at another time.

Taking it further
● Paint letter shapes, using big movements. Use a large paintbrush and a bucket of water to paint them on an outside wall.
● Have paper and pencils handy and try writing the letters after forming them in the salt tray.

LEARNING OPPORTUNITY
● To choose the correct letter for the first sound in simple words.

YOU WILL NEED
12 cards, approximately 8cm x 8cm; pen.

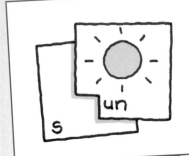

 STEPPING STONE
Hear and say the initial sound in words and know which letters represent some of the sounds.

EARLY LEARNING GOAL
Communication, language and literacy: Link sounds to letters, naming and sounding the letters of the alphabet.

Find the beginning

Sharing the game
● Cut a 2.5cm square from the bottom left corner of six cards. Draw a picture on the top half of these cards, illustrating a simple three-letter word, for example, a cat, hat, dog, sun, bin, leg and so on.
● Place each cut card on top of an uncut one. Write the word corresponding to the picture, with the first letter in the bottom left corner of the underneath card and the last two letters on the cut card, immediately to the right of the cut-out square. Make sure that the letters are evenly spaced (see illustration, left).
● Show your child the cut cards, with the pictures and word endings. Show her that the first letter is missing from the words. Invite her to try to find the missing letters.
● Hand her one picture card and ask what the picture shows. Encourage her to tell you the first sound.
● Spread the initial-letter cards on the table and ask your child if she can place the picture card on top of the card with the letter that writes the missing sound.
● Work through the cards, until each one has been matched to its missing initial letter.

Taking it further
● Add to the cards. You will find that you can use the same initial-letter card for a number of pictures.
● Use the same idea, but this time cut out a square at the bottom right of the picture card, and make end-sound cards with letters in the bottom right corner of the other cards.

LEARNING OPPORTUNITY
● To begin to spell and write simple words.

YOU WILL NEED
A set of 26 home-made alphabet cards; set of word-ending cards (see page 127).

🥾 **STEPPING STONE**
Continue a rhyming string.

⭐ **EARLY LEARNING GOAL**
Communication, language and literacy: Use their phonic knowledge to write simple regular words.

Changing words

Sharing the game
● Show your child the different cards and explain that you are going to explain to him how to write some words and how to change one word into another.

● Take the at ending card and place it on the table. Say, 'This says "a-t", "at". If I put this letter (pick up the "c" card) in front of it, I can make the word "c-a-t-", "cat"'. Place the 'c' card in front of the ending.
● Now say, 'The word "bat" rhymes with "cat". They both sound the same at the end. Only the beginning is different. To change "cat" into "bat", I only need to change the beginning letter'. Pick up the 'b' card and replace the 'c' card.
● Ask your child if he can change the word to 'rat' by putting a different letter at the beginning. Work through as many rhyming words as your child is happy to make, using the list on page 127.
● Begin the game again, using a different word ending.

Taking it further
● Rather than suggesting words to make, ask your child to think of a rhyming word and then to build it.
● Help your child to write a list of the words as he builds them. Depending on his stage of development, either write the endings for him and let him just write the initial letter, or help him to write the complete word.

● To use writing to create a book.

YOU WILL NEED
A piece of paper 45cm x 115cm; pencils; felt-tipped pens or colouring crayons.

 STEPPING STONE
Use writing as a means of recording and communicating.

 EARLY LEARNING GOAL
Communication, language and literacy: Attempt writing for different purposes.

Time to dress

Sharing the game
● Fold the piece of paper into equal-sized zigzags. Turn the paper so that the first page will open in the same direction as an ordinary book. Show it to your child, inviting her to help you make it into her own special book.
● Write the title on the front page, including your child's name, for example, 'Rosie gets dressed'. Explain to your child that it is going to be a book about her getting ready in the morning.

● Draw a figure like the one shown above on each page of the book. Suggest to your child that she draw hair on each figure to make it look like her.
● Talk about getting dressed, and ask her what she puts on first each morning. Ask her to draw that item of clothing on the figure on the first page. Underneath the figure, write, 'Every morning Rosie puts on her ____ first'. Help your child to write in her name and the appropriate word, or write it for her.
● Continue through the book, adding items of clothing to the figures, finishing with a fully clothed figure. Add captions, such as, 'Next, I put on ____', 'After that, I put on ____', and so on.

Taking it further
● Make other books about your child's day or her week. Encourage her to suggest the words that she would like to be written on each page and write them for her, or help her to write them. Try encouraging her to write the first letter of some words, followed by a line, then fill in the remainder of the word.

CHAPTER 6

LET'S FIND OUT

To learn effectively, young children need opportunities to express ideas, to put ideas to the test, and to modify them in the light of their experience. Language skills are vital tools in this voyage of discovery. When children are allowed to experiment in this way, discussing what is happening as they do so, they utilise and develop a range of language skills that will prove essential in every area of the school curriculum: the ability to organise their thoughts and to reason; the ability to make predictions; and, very importantly, the skill of working through errors to further their learning.

PROMOTING REASONING SKILLS

For successful learning to take place, children need to store ideas in an orderly way. It is also important for them to be able to put their ideas across to others. As children reason through ideas, they organise and review what they already know. They sort through their knowledge, before storing new information, or in order to plan what they want to say. In other words, they engage in a sort of mental filing process. As they reason through their ideas with others, children practise and perfect their communication skills. In helping children to develop good reasoning skills, we, therefore, enable them to become more efficient as learners and effective communicators.

How you can help

● Provide a good model for your child by supplying reasons when you ask him to do something. If you ask him to wear his raincoat, explain, for example, that you have heard the weather forecast, which has said that it might rain and that it is already very cloudy outside.

● Encourage your child to give reasons for his statements. Ask if he can explain why he does not want to eat his broccoli. Is it because he is not hungry, or because he does not like the taste, or the feel of it in his mouth. Explain that it will help you to know the reason.

● Acknowledge and respect your child's reasoning, even if you do not agree with it. Say that you can understand that he does not want to go to bed, but that he has to be up early tomorrow, and that you know that it will be more difficult for him to get up if he goes to bed late.

● Encourage discussions about anything and everything, showing pleasure in your child's ability to suggest reasons for his thinking.

● Play 'Silly reasons', making up silly reasons, for example, why your child should wear a hat.

ENCOURAGING PREDICTION SKILLS

The learning process is a cycle. Children embark on any new learning with a certain amount of knowledge already in place. Linking new knowledge with what they already know makes for more effective learning. The ability to predict what might come next and to guess the outcome of any action, requires children to look at what they already know and to open their minds to a range of possibilities. This makes efficient use of what is already known and helps to prepare the mind to acquire new information. It is an important skill for many areas of learning. For example, children utilise this skill constantly when they read, and it is of major importance in science and mathematics. As children compare their predictions with what they see or hear, they consolidate old information and add new. This new information, in turn, becomes part of their body of knowledge, and it is from this enhanced base that they will embark on their next learning task.

How you can help
● Pause when you are reading stories to your child and ask what she thinks might happen next. Encourage discussion of different possibilities.
● Involve your child in the planning of family events, encouraging her to look ahead and make suggestions of things to do and items needed to make for a successful event. Let her help with packing for a holiday, or to make invitations for a birthday party.
● Talk through planned outings and encourage your child to anticipate what might happen and what she might see.
● Help your child to make links which will enable her to make appropriate predictions, by supplying relevant information. Say, for example, 'We need to ask someone to water the plants when we are away. Plants need water to grow. What do you think will happen to ours if someone doesn't water them?'.

PROVIDING OPPORTUNITIES FOR EXPERIMENTATION

An ideal learning opportunity for young children will allow them to try out an idea, to discuss what is happening, and to compare the outcome with their expectations. Young children need to be given the chance to experiment. Making errors is an inherent part of this learning process. Having an idea or a prediction proved correct will consolidate what is already known. A mistake, properly handled, moves the child forward in his learning. A supportive adult can help him to understand that, in making such a mistake and reasoning through what went wrong and what to try next, he really learns something new.

How you can help
● Provide plenty of opportunities for your child to experiment with natural materials, such as sand and water, and be available to discuss things, if needed. Accept that messiness is a necessary part of learning.
● Respond positively to your child's attempts to use things for unconventional purposes. If your child is trying to build a tower with items that are precious to you, try to offer substitutes, rather than stopping the activity. Praise his inventiveness.
● Do not be too keen to always jump in and show him how to do something or to explain the probable outcome of his experiments. Let him have the joy of discovering things himself and show a real interest when he does.
● Accept that making mistakes is part of learning and help your child to see mistakes as stepping-stones. If he has made a wrong prediction about something, say, for example, 'Never mind. It was a really good idea, and in trying it out you've learnt something new, haven't you?'.
● Explain to your child that it is just as important to ask the right questions and try things out, as to be right.
● As part of the bedtime routine, ask your child if there is a question for which he would like to know the answer. Suggest that you try to find it out the next day and do just that.

LET'S FIND OUT

LEARNING OPPORTUNITY
● To learn vocabulary that will be needed for maths.

YOU WILL NEED
A selection of plastic containers (wide-necked ones are best); plastic jug; sink or bowl of water; waterproof aprons.

STEPPING STONE
Build up vocabulary that reflects the breadth of their experiences.

EARLY LEARNING GOAL
Communication, language and literacy: Extend their vocabulary, exploring the meanings and sounds of new words.

Make a splash

Sharing the game
● Show your child the bowl of water and the containers. Explain to her that you are going to play a game to find out how much water the containers will hold.
● Hand her the jug and one of the larger containers. Ask her to put some water in the jug, and to use it to fill the container. Explain that you

would like her to fill the container right to the top. As she pours, comment on the stage that she has reached. Say, for example, 'Now the container is half-full. You'll need to pour some more water into it'.
● When the container is full, hand her a second smaller container. Ask, 'Do you think this container will hold as much water as that one?'. Suggest that you find out by pouring the water from the larger container into the smaller one.
● When the smaller container is full, and there is still water in the larger one, comment that, 'The big container can hold more than the smaller one. The smaller one holds less'.
● Ask your child to empty both containers and to choose two more. Compare different containers in this way, emphasising words and phrases such as 'empty', 'full', 'half-full', 'more than' and 'less than'.

Taking it further
● Help your child to try to grade several containers, lining them up to show which holds 'most' and which holds 'least'.

LEARNING OPPORTUNITY
● To listen to and to enjoy responding to conversation.

YOU WILL NEED
Pictures of a wide range of items that can be purchased in a variety of shops (optional).

 STEPPING STONE
Listen to others in one-to-one/small groups when conversation interests them.

 EARLY LEARNING GOAL
Communication, language and literacy: Enjoy listening to and using spoken and written language, and readily turn to it in their play and learning.

Where should I go?

Sharing the game
● Invite your child to play a game in which he has to work out where you could buy different things.
● Choose a picture of a toy, for example, and show it to your child. Say, 'Do you know, where I should go to buy a toy?'. If he gives the answer, 'A toy shop', ask if he can think of any other places to buy toys. Give clues, if necessary. Toys can also be bought, for example, at supermarkets, post offices, card shops and newsagents.

● Now let your child choose a picture and ask you if you know where to go to buy the item.
● You do not need pictures to play this game. You can simply name the items. However, pictures help a child to key in to the idea.
● Encourage your child to think of as many different places as possible to buy the various items, using the opportunity to introduce names of specialist shops, such as 'greengrocer's', 'chemist's' and so on.

Taking it further
● Follow up the game with a visit to local shops, to see how many of them stock a particular item.
● Rather than asking your child if he knows where to go to buy an item, try asking where it comes from, encouraging him to link wool items with sheep, eggs with hens, bread with wheat, and so on, rather than simply with supermarkets.

LEARNING OPPORTUNITY
● To listen attentively to stories, and to remember a story line.

YOU WILL NEED
Sheets of paper; white wax crayon or white candle; watery paint; paintbrush.

 STEPPING STONE
Listen to stories with increasing attention and recall.

★ **EARLY LEARNING GOAL**
Communication, language and literacy: Listen with enjoyment, and respond to stories, and make up their own stories.

Just like magic

Sharing the game
● Use the wax crayon, or candle, to make five 'invisible' drawings for the story below (see illustration, left) on five sheets of paper. Draw thick lines. Keep them in order.
● Invite your child to listen to a story. Hand her the paintbrush, telling her that it is a 'magic' brush. Say that you will tell her how you got it.
● Tell the story below, pausing as indicated. Each time you pause, tell your child to paint over the next sheet of paper with the paint. Say that the pictures for the story will appear 'like magic'.

'I was out for a walk one day, when, suddenly, I came upon a (*pause*) forest. I walked into the forest, and there, inside, was a (*pause*) tiny cottage. In the garden grew beautiful (*pause*) flowers. As I stood looking at the flowers, I heard a loud "Miaow" above my head. I looked up, and saw a (*pause*) cat. It was stuck in a tree. I scrambled up the tree to rescue it. I had just got it down, when the door of the cottage opened, and out came a (*pause*) magician. "You've rescued my cat," he said. "I must give you a reward." And that is how I got my magic paintbrush.'

● Ask if your child can remember the story. Encourage her to use the pictures to help her to retell it.

Taking it further
● Encourage your child to make up other simple stories, and draw 'magic' pictures for her to help her retell them to you.

LEARNING OPPORTUNITY
● To predict how sentences in a rhyme might end and to make up the ending to a story.

YOU WILL NEED
Just you and your child.

STEPPING STONE
Suggest how the story might end.

EARLY LEARNING GOAL
Communication, language and literacy: Explore and experiment with sounds, words and texts.

Aliens

Sharing the game
● Invite your child to come and listen to a rhyme. Explain that some of the rhyming words are missing, and that you would like him to tell you what he thinks they might be. Say that some, but not all, of the missing words are numbers.
● Read the rhyme to your child, leaving out the words in italics, or saying only the first sound to give a clue, if necessary.

Two little aliens landed on the moon.
One flew off again and said,
'I'll be back *soon*.'

He brought along a friend, to come and see
What the moon looked like,
So then there were *three*.

Two little aliens said, 'This is fun!
We'll go home and get some other friends.'
So that left *one*.

One little alien saw his four friends arrive.
He waved and gave a great big grin,
So that made *five*.

Three little aliens said, 'There isn't much to do,'
And jumped back in their spaceship,
So that left *two*.

Two little aliens wondered whether they should stay,
But decided to go home
And come again another *day*.

● Now ask your child to tell you what he thinks happened, when the aliens went back to the moon on another day. Did they take a picnic, or games to play? Did they have fun?

Taking it further
● Make up other stories about the five little aliens and their visits to earth. Start with a story about them visiting you, and make your child the person who opens the door to them. Let him say what happens.

LEARNING
OPPORTUNITY
● To ask questions, and
suggest explanations for
why things happen.

YOU WILL NEED
Four pieces of the same
cloth (or similar socks);
sink; washing powder;
outdoor washing line.

STEPPING STONE
Question why
things happen, and give
explanations.

EARLY LEARNING
GOAL
**Communication,
language and literacy:**
Sustain attentive
listening, responding to
what they have heard by
relevant comments,
questions or actions.

Wash day

Sharing the game
● Ask your child to
help with an
experiment to find the
best place to hang up
clothes so that they
dry quickly.
● Suggest that she
wash a number of
pieces of the same
cloth and hang them
in different places.
Ask why she thinks it
is important to use
the same cloth in
each place.
● Wash the cloths,
together. As you do

so, ask your child to think of different places to hang them up. Help
her, by making suggestions, if necessary, such as laying one cloth in a
shady place outside, as well as putting one on the line.
● Let your child put the cloths in place. After an hour or two, ask her
to check how dry they are. As she examines each cloth, ask her why
she thinks it has dried well, or not, in the place she left it. Discuss
whether the cloth on the line would always dry well, or if the weather
might make a difference. Encourage your child to think about factors,
such as heat and wind, and whether the cloths have been laid flat or
hung up.

Taking it further
● Encourage your child to question why things happen by using
sticky labels to make some 'Good question!' badges. Draw a question
mark on the badge with coloured rays around it. Award a badge each
time your child shows curiosity in why or how something happens.
Help her to find out the answers to her questions, at your local library
or by using the Internet.

LET'S FIND OUT

LEARNING OPPORTUNITY
● To begin to understand how different conditions can bring about different results.

YOU WILL NEED
A tray of ice cubes; saucers; any book that features a story about snow and ice, or a non-fiction book about cold places (optional).

 STEPPING STONE Begin to make patterns in their experience through linking cause and effect.

EARLY LEARNING GOAL Communication, language and literacy: Use talk to clarify thinking and ideas.

Freezing fun

Sharing the game
● Invite your child to join you in carrying out some experiments with ice cubes. Explain that you are going to try to find out where an ice cube would melt quickest.

● Help your child to put an ice cube on each of the saucers, and ask him to put the saucers in different places. Talk to him about what makes an ice cube melt, and try to encourage him to think about placing the saucers in positions where the temperature would vary. Suggest, for example, leaving one near a radiator, one in a fridge, a third on a table and a fourth outside. Encourage your child to talk about the effect this might have on different cubes.
● Leave the ice cubes for an hour. Meanwhile, share the story-book or non-fiction book, and use it as a focus for talking about cold places and activities that can be carried out in snowy and icy conditions.
● Return to check the ice cubes periodically, comparing how much they have melted. Talk about the link between warmth and melting.
● After an hour, check the ice cubes again, and ask him why he thinks that one (or more) has melted more quickly or slowly than the rest.

Taking it further
● Talk about ways in which you could speed up the melting process.
● Talk about frozen food and why we let it thaw before cooking or increase the cooking time to make sure that it is cooked properly.

LEARNING OPPORTUNITY
● To predict the outcome of an action, to test the prediction, and to talk about what happens.

YOU WILL NEED
A bowl or a sink of water; two pieces of paper; pencil; two plastic straws; sticky tape; two lumps of Plasticine; plastic cloth; selection of heavy and light objects, such as a feather, an apple, a grape (or marble), a small piece of wood, a spoon, a piece of orange peel (try to ensure an equal number of 'floaters' and 'sinkers').

 STEPPING STONE Use talk to connect ideas, explain what is happening and anticipate what might happen next.

EARLY LEARNING GOAL
Communication, language and literacy: Use talk to organise and clarify thinking.

Sink or swim?

Sharing the game
● On one piece of paper, draw a boat floating on water. On the other, draw one that has sunk beneath the water. Make two flags using the paper, sticky tape and the straws. Place them on the plastic cloth, using the Plasticine to anchor them.

● Invite your child to play a floating and sinking game. Ask if she would like to be captain of the 'floaters' or the 'sinkers'.
● Let your child choose an item for her team. Encourage her to give reasons for her choice. Tell her to test the object in the water. If it does belong to her team, she places it under her flag. If not, you win the item.
● Take it in turns to choose items in this way, predicting what they will do in the water. Small items such as a grape or marble may confuse your child. Encourage her to pick them up, to feel the weight of them.

Taking it further
● Use a different selection of items that need more detailed reasoning, such as a yoghurt pot with holes in it, a piece of cloth, an ice cube, and so on.

YOU WILL NEED
Two empty cereal boxes; sticky tape; a cupful of each of four different pulses and grains of varying size, for example, rice, lentils, chickpeas and butter beans; plain paper; paint.

STEPPING STONE
Use talk to explain what is happening and anticipate what might happen next.

EARLY LEARNING GOAL
Communication, language and literacy: Use talk to clarify thinking.

Sea in a box

Sharing the game

● Tell your child that you are going to show him how to capture the sound of the sea in a box.

● Invite him to place a small handful of each of the items into one of the empty cereal boxes. Seal the box securely with sticky tape.

● Ask your child to hold the box at both ends and to slowly lower one hand, so that the box begins to tilt slowly, to produce a sound like waves on a beach (you may need to help him). Listen to the sound together.

● Ask what he thinks is happening to the items inside the box. Which one does he think will move most quickly from one end of the box to the other? Test out his answers by trying each different item, one at a time, in the other empty box.

● Help your child to cover the 'sea box' with plain paper and let him paint waves on it.

Taking it further

● Try letting toy cars roll down a board or tray propped on a slope. Predict whether the lighter or heavier cars will reach the bottom first.

● Place two objects in front of your child and ask him which will be heavier to pick up. Make sure that the larger object is not always the heavier. Try a bag of sugar and a cardboard box. Let your child test his answer by picking up the objects.

LEARNING OPPORTUNITY
● To talk about what might happen when certain actions are carried out.

YOU WILL NEED
Blue and yellow paint; food colouring; water; plastic glass; packet of jelly; small bowl; top of a carrot; saucer.

STEPPING STONE
Use talk to anticipate what might happen next.

EARLY LEARNING GOAL
Communication, language and literacy: Use talk to clarify ideas.

What will happen?

Sharing the game
● Ask your child if she would like to play a 'thinking' game with you. Explain that you are going to ask her what she thinks will happen if you do certain things. Tell her that, when she has told you, she can watch what you do to see if she was right.
● Now ask these questions, waiting for your child's answer and carrying out the relevant action after asking each question:

'What do you think will happen if I mix the blue paint with the yellow paint?'
'What do you think will happen if I add one drop of this food colouring to this glass of water?'
'What do you think will happen if I pour hot water on to these jelly cubes?'.

● Encourage your child to describe what she is seeing, as she watches what actually happens.
● Finally, ask what she thinks will happen if you put the carrot top on the saucer, with a little water. Explain that it is something that she will need to wait a few days to see. Encourage her to check the saucer each day and to make sure that there is always a little water in it.

Taking it further
● Experiment with mixing other paint colours.
● Ask questions which encourage your child to really use her imagination. Try, 'What do you think would happen if we had wings like birds?' or 'What do you think would happen if it never rained?'.

LEARNING OPPORTUNITY
● To suggest reasons why certain everyday events occur, and which circumstances may affect these events.

YOU WILL NEED
A piece of cloth; piece of kitchen roll; plate; cotton wool; piece of aluminium foil; half a cup of flour; sink; jug; plastic tray.

 STEPPING STONE
Use talk to connect ideas, explain what is happening and anticipate what might happen next.

 EARLY LEARNING GOAL
Communication, language and literacy: Use talk to organise and clarify thinking.

Rain, rain go away

Sharing the game
● This is a good game to play on a rainy day. Ask your child where he thinks all the rain goes, when it falls. Listen to his answer, and invite him to try some experiments with you, to find out.
● Explain that he is going to pour a little water on to different materials to see what will happen. Say that, with some materials the water will

disappear, and with others, it will not.
● Show him the materials. Ask him to choose one, to place on the plastic tray first and encourage him to guess whether the water will disappear.
● Put a small amount of water into the jug and let your child pour it on to his chosen material. Talk about it soaking the water up, or not, and about puddles forming in the tray. Ask whether the material is hard, smooth or soft. Encourage him to compare the next material with the first and to predict what will happen.
● Work through all the materials, encouraging your child to make links between the feel of materials and their ability to soak up water.
● Let him pour water into the sink and watch it run down the drain.
● Now talk about different materials outside, such as soil, concrete and paving stones, and about where we see puddles. Talk about drains as well. Ask again where he thinks all the rain goes.

Taking it further
● Help your child to test his new conclusions by going for a puddle-spotting walk in the rain, to check where puddles form and how soil gets wet, and to watch water disappearing down drains.
● Let him try pouring a larger amount of water on to the cotton wool, flour and so on to see if there is a limit to the amount they soak up.
● Use the word 'absorb' and explain that it is a special word for soaking up liquids such as water.

LEARNING OPPORTUNITY
● To make lists to record observations from an experiment.

YOU WILL NEED
Paper; pencils; selection of light, medium-weight and heavier objects (a feather, leaf, paper clip and paper tissue make good light objects); newspaper.

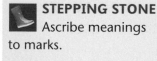

STEPPING STONE
Ascribe meanings to marks.

EARLY LEARNING GOAL
Communication, language and literacy: Attempt writing for different purposes, using features of different forms such as lists.

Windy weather

Sharing the game
● A windy day is a good time to play this game. Invite your child to help you with an experiment to find out which things would be blown about by the wind.
● Draw a line down the middle of a piece of paper. Draw a flag, blowing in the wind, at the top of one column, and a limp flag at the top of the other. Explain to your child that she is going to make a list of the things that blow in the wind, and a list of those that do not.

● Say that she is going to make the wind by blowing hard, to see which things she can move. Encourage her to look at the items that you have laid out for the experiment, and to predict which she might be able to move. Let her try one item at a time.
● Ask her to record the item in the correct column, either by drawing a picture, writing the first letter or attempting to write the word, depending on her stage of development.
● Try making a stronger wind by waving newspaper behind items, to see if this makes a difference.

Taking it further
● Set up a simple flag outside, or a ready-made pinwheel. Keep a weather chart for a week, encouraging your child to record the strength of the wind with the following symbols:
0 no wind   )) slight breeze   ))) wind   )))) strong wind.

LEARNING OPPORTUNITY
● To learn how to form some letters that have a common shape.

YOU WILL NEED
Sheets of A4 paper; black marker pen; tracing paper.

Letter match

Sharing the game
● On one sheet of paper write the first set of letters, as illustrated (see right). Write them clearly, using guidelines so that the bodies of the letters are the same height.

● Take a small square of tracing paper and trace over the letter 'c'. Invite your child to come and find out something about the letters.

● Ask your child to put the tracing paper letter on top of the one on the A4 sheet that is exactly the same. Make sure that he is holding the tracing paper the right way around.

● When your child has placed the traced letter correctly, explain that this is the shape you begin with, to write all the letters on the page. Help him to see this by placing the 'c' on each letter in turn.

● Draw a faint letter 'c' on another sheet of paper. Ask your child to write over it. Draw another faint 'c'. Ask him to write over it, then keep going round to make an 'o'. Start each letter from the sheet in this way.

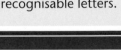

● Repeat the game, using the letter 'r' as the common shape (see left). Point out that, to write these letters, we do not always start with an exact 'r' shape, but that we do have to make the same down, up and over movement at the start of the letter.

Taking it further
● Encourage your child to make 'labels' with the above letters on them, and to find one object that begins with the sound that each letter makes. Ask him to place the labels on the appropriate objects.

🥾 **STEPPING STONE**
Begin to form recognisable letters.

⭐ **EARLY LEARNING GOAL**
Communication, language and literacy: Use a pencil and hold it effectively to form recognisable letters.

PUZZLE IT OUT

Language is the framework around which children construct their thinking. Effective thinking skills require children to be able to sequence (to put thoughts into a logical, correct order), to clarify their ideas through talking about them, and to make links between one statement and another. Children also need to be able to draw conclusions from available information. Such information can come from a range of sources, such as their own senses, discussion with others and books and stories. The more practice they are given in talking through and organising information, the more skilled their thinking becomes.

DEVELOPING SEQUENCING AND ORDERING SKILLS

The ability to sequence and order information and thoughts and to see patterns in their experience is a skill which underpins many areas of learning. In mathematics, it enables young children to count, to compare items in size, weight, height and length, and to understand concepts such as multiplication and times tables. In English, it is essential that children can organise their thoughts into logical, sequential order if they are to produce well-structured pieces of writing. In history, this enables them to comprehend sequences of events. To assist children in developing these skills, we need to give them strategies for organising their language and, as a result, their thinking.

How you can help

● Use two sets of coloured cardboard or plastic shapes and lay out a sequence with one set, out of sight of your child (behind a large book). Describe the sequence in which you have laid out the shapes, asking your child to lay out her shapes in the same order. Remove the book and compare the two sets. Ask your child to create a new sequence and to give you instructions.

● Say a simple sentence, jumbling the order of the words, for example, 'boy the sweets likes', and ask your child to put the words into the correct order to make a sensible sentence.

● Ask your child to describe a simple everyday event, step by step, as though she was describing it to a visitor from outer space.

● Make simple three-picture stories of events such as a plant growing. Present the pictures to your child out of sequence, and ask her to put them in the correct order to tell a story.

● Create opportunities to compare the size of everyday items, such as shoes. Line up a row of wellington boots in size order.

● Provide practical opportunities to help your child understand vocabulary such as 'more', 'less' and 'most'. Let her help with cooking activities, for

How you can help

● Make riddles a part of your regular routine, and encourage your child to make up riddles for you.

● Play rhyming riddles such as, 'You wear it on your head and it rhymes with cat'.

● Make up a sentence with one word missing and see how many different words that would make sense your child can fit into the sentence. Try, 'My friend ____ to the shops to buy some bread'. Encourage suggestions such as 'went' and 'ran'. Then look for words that would make silly sentences, such as 'hopped', 'crawled' and 'cart-wheeled'.

● Share jokes together that encourage children to think about different words. Make them appropriate for the age of your child, for example, 'Why are a dog and a tree alike? Because they both have a bark'.

● As your child begins to recognise simple words for reading, make a collection of pictures of everyday items from magazines. Choose a picture for a simple word that he cannot yet read. Hide the picture somewhere in the room, and write the relevant word on a piece of card. Give the word to your child, encouraging him to think about the sound of the first letter, and to make suggestions for the word. Send him to hunt the picture to find out what the word actually says.

Younger children will find it easier to think through activities that are multisensory. As they pass through the Foundation Stage, children will begin to be able to enjoy games that are solely language-based, such as riddles. It is advisable to defer challenges that are well beyond the ability of children at a given stage of development and which could run the risk of demoralising them.

How you can help

● Use questions to help your child tap into what she already knows on a subject, before embarking on an activity.

● Never run the risk of your child thinking that your approval depends on her winning a game or completing a task successfully.

● Know when to stop playing a game. Do not be tempted to push on beyond the point when your child is showing signs of tiring, even if the game has gone well up until that point.

example, and talk about needing to add more of an ingredient, or putting a little less on the scales. Cooking also provides experience of following a set of instructions in the correct sequence.

USING WORD GAMES

The use of word games provides an effective method of helping young children develop their language for thinking. Word games are, by nature, an interactive method of learning. They allow for the possibility of a quick, flexible response to children's learning needs. An adult, engaged in a game of riddles, for example, can present a more challenging example to a child who has clearly mastered the first examples with ease. Alternatively, the adult can offer support for a child's thinking by asking appropriate questions to help him work out a correct answer. Word games also offer the opportunity for word play and humour, both of which are powerful tools in engaging the attention of young children.

SETTING APPROPRIATE CHALLENGES

Children who are provided with opportunities to experience success in using their thinking skills will grow in confidence and be encouraged to use those skills again. To develop their skills children need challenges that allow them to utilise what they already know to take them a step further.

Smaller or bigger?

LEARNING OPPORTUNITY
● To use talk to describe actions and to make a train of thought clear.

YOU WILL NEED
A collection of any household objects or toys that come in a variety of sizes, for example spoons, building blocks, teddy bears and several glasses filled with increasing amounts of water.

Sharing the game

● Lay out the collection of objects on a table, and explain to your child that you are going to play a sorting game. Say that you are going to ask him to arrange the groups of objects in rows to show which is the smallest and which is the biggest, or which is the shortest and which is the tallest.

● Gather together all the objects of the same type, for example, the building blocks. Ask your child to place the blocks in a row. Say, 'Start on this side with the shortest. Then put one after another, with each one getting taller, until you finish with the tallest on this other side. It should look like stairs when you have finished'.

● As your child works, encourage him to tell you which object he is going to choose to put in place next and why.

● Work through different sets of objects in this way, sometimes beginning with the smallest, and sometimes with the biggest. Use words such as 'longer' and 'shorter', and 'fuller' and 'emptier', for example, with the glasses.

Taking it further

● Use playing cards to encourage your child to sort them into number sequence.

● Ask your child to draw pictures of members of the family, placing them across the page in height order, or in age order.

 STEPPING STONE
Talk activities through, reflecting on and modifying what they are doing.

 EARLY LEARNING GOAL
Communication, language and literacy: Use talk to organise, sequence and clarify thinking.

LEARNING OPPORTUNITY
● To describe familiar objects, on the basis of feel, discriminating between one object and another.

YOU WILL NEED
A cardboard box; tape; craft knife; objects that are familiar to your child, such as a toy; toothbrush; spoon; crayon; plastic cup.

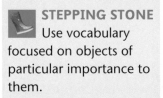

STEPPING STONE
Use vocabulary focused on objects of particular importance to them.

EARLY LEARNING GOAL
Communication, language and literacy: Extend their vocabulary, exploring the meanings and sounds of new words.

Feel and say

Sharing the game
● Use the craft knife to cut a hole in either side of the box. Check that the holes are large enough (approximately 10cm) for your child's hand to pass through. Tape the top of the box closed. Place your chosen objects inside the box.

● Invite your child to play a guessing game with you. Explain that there are a number of objects in the box. Say that they are all things that she sees around her every day.
● Next, ask your child to put her hands through the holes in the box, pick up an object, and try to tell you what it is. Ask her to describe to you exactly what she can feel, before she tries to guess what it could be. Question her about the shape of the object, its length, whether it feels the same all over, and so on. Then suggest that she tell you what she thinks it could be.
● Let her pull the object out of the box to check her guess, and then begin again with another item.

Taking it further
● Place a number of toys in the box, including one that is a favourite of your child. Invite her to find the favourite, describing it by its feel, and saying why the other toys cannot be the one she is looking for.

LEARNING OPPORTUNITY
● To use a wide range of words to give clues for a riddle.

YOU WILL NEED
Just you and your child.

 STEPPING STONE Use a widening range of words to express or elaborate ideas.

EARLY LEARNING GOAL Speak clearly and audibly with confidence and control and show awareness of the listener.

What is...?

Sharing the game

● Invite your child to play a game of riddles. Explain that you are going to think of an object. Say that you will describe the thing as carefully as you can, and that you may say what it looks, feels, tastes, smells or sounds like. Tell your child that this will give him clues, and that he must try to guess what you are thinking of.

● Make your first clue quite easy, saying:
'What feels soft and furry, has whiskers and says, "Miaow"?'.

● When your child has guessed the answer, try some of these riddles:
'What is yellow, spreads on bread and tastes greasy?'
'What feels wet, smells fresh and clean, and makes bubbles in water?'
'Which fruit is round, tastes juicy and has the same name as its colour?'
'What has numbers on buttons to press and goes "brrrr, brrrr"?'.

● When your child has got the idea, suggest that you take it in turns to give the clues. If he finds it difficult to give appropriate clues, help him to formulate them by asking questions such as, 'What colour is it?', 'Does it feel hard or soft?', 'Does it make a noise?' and 'Does it taste sweet or sour?'.

Taking it further

● Rather than giving clues for an object, suggest that your child has to ask questions to try to find out what it is. To begin with, tell him the category of object, for example, 'I am thinking of a vegetable'. Later encourage him to ask first of all if it is a fruit, vegetable, animal and so on.

LEARNING OPPORTUNITY
● To use a range of vocabulary to describe the texture of materials.

YOU WILL NEED
Two cardboard boxes; two small pieces of various textured materials (kitchen foil, tissue paper, sandpaper, plastic cut from carriers, fabrics).

 STEPPING STONE
Use a widening range of words to express or elaborate ideas.

EARLY LEARNING GOAL
Communication, language and literacy: Speak clearly and audibly with confidence and control and show awareness of the listener.

Two of a kind

Sharing the game
● Place one piece of each material in each box, mixing the different pieces together well.
● Invite your child to try to find two pieces of the same material, one from each box. Explain that she must do this without looking at either of the two pieces of material.

● Let your child sit with a box on either side of her. Ask her to put her hand into one box and to choose a piece of material. When she has chosen, tell her to feel the material and to describe it to you. Prompt her with questions if necessary, using words such as 'rough', 'slippery', 'hard', 'smooth', 'soft', 'velvety' and so on.

● Next, ask her to put her hand into the other box and to feel for a piece of material that is exactly the same as the first one she chose. Remind her of the words that she used to describe the first piece and ask her if the piece that she is touching feels the same.
● Repeat the game, until all the pieces are paired.

Taking it further
● Choose different household objects and take it in turns to describe them, talking about the colour, the shape, the feel, the weight and so on. See who can keep talking about one object for the longest time.

PUZZLE IT OUT

Bird's eye view

Sharing the game

● Make simple line drawings of the mug, jug, bottle and teapot from a bird's eye view. Use the illustrations on this page to help you.

● Place the four objects and the four drawings on the table, with the drawings jumbled up, so that they are not beside the relevant objects.

● Invite your child to play a game with you. Explain that you have drawn some pictures of the four things on the table. Say that you have not drawn them in the usual way, but as if you were a bird, flying over them.

● Ask your child to try to work out which picture goes with which object. Say that he might need to look at the things on the table from above to help him.

● Now hand him the picture of the teapot. Ask him to tell you what he sees in the picture. Encourage him to notice the two things sticking out from the circle on either side, and the small circle in the middle of the bigger one.

● Next, let him look down on the four objects on the table. Ask if one of them has two things sticking out on either side.

● Work through the pictures in this way, encouraging him to look closely at detail in the pictures and on the objects, until he has matched all four pictures and objects.

Taking it further

● Try drawing other items in this way. Choose things that he will not be able to view from above, but will need to imagine, such as a tree or a house.

LEARNING OPPORTUNITY
● To use simple sentences to talk through their thinking.

YOU WILL NEED
A plastic bottle; mug; jug; teapot; paper; pencil.

STEPPING STONE
Use simple grammatical structures.

EARLY LEARNING GOAL
Communication, language and literacy: Interact with others, taking turns in conversation.

LEARNING OPPORTUNITY
● To use more complex sentences to state reasons.

YOU WILL NEED
A door key; glass; pen with a lid; access to a tap.

What's going wrong?

Sharing the game
● Tell your child that you are having a very annoying day, because things keep going wrong. Ask her if she could try to help you to sort things out.
● Explain that you have been trying to lock the door, but that you do not seem to be able to do it. Show her how you put the key in the door, but insert the wrong end of the key. Say that you tried to turn the key, but it is not working. Ask if she can think why not.

● If your child has difficulty in spotting the problem, draw attention to it by asking appropriate questions. Give praise when she supplies the reason.
● Now ask for help with other problems. Try filling the glass with water from the tap, but turn the tap the wrong way.
● Next, explain that your pen is not working properly, and try writing with the lid still on.
● Each time that your child provides you with a reason, repeat it back to her, linking it with the original problem. Say, for example, 'Oh, I understand now. I can't get a drink of water because I'm turning the tap the wrong way'.

Taking it further
● Use pictures from magazines as a focus for a game of 'Why?'. Show your child a picture of a girl in a summer dress and ask why she might be upset if it rained. Choose a picture of a clean kitchen, and ask why it would not be a good idea to let the dog walk through it with muddy feet.

 STEPPING STONE
Begin to use more complex sentences.

EARLY LEARNING GOAL
Communication, language and literacy: Speak clearly and audibly with control and show awareness of the listener.

LEARNING OPPORTUNITY
● To link what they know to what they see and hear happening.

YOU WILL NEED
Small handfuls of rice, buttons, marbles (or dice) and paper clips; empty cocoa tin; tea towel.

THINK FIRST!
Be aware of the dangers of choking and never allow your child to put small items in his mouth or to play unsupervised.

STEPPING STONE
Use talk to connect ideas, explain what is happening and anticipate what might happen next.

EARLY LEARNING GOAL
Communication, language and literacy: Use talk to organise and clarify thinking.

What's inside?

Sharing the game

● Show your child the rice, buttons, paper clips and marbles, explaining that these are going to be used for a game. As you look at each in turn, encourage him to feel them and to talk about them. Ask him whether the items feel heavy or light. Let him rub the rice grains between his fingers and ask whether they make a noise as they move against each other. Encourage him to tell you whether the noise is a quiet or a loud one. Let him run one marble into another and ask him to tell you about the noise they make.

● When your child has explored the various items, explain that you are going to ask him to close his eyes while you put one of them into the cocoa tin. When you have done this, place the lid on the tin and cover the remaining items with the tea towel, so that it is not obvious what is missing.

● Let your child shake the cocoa tin. Ask him to describe the noise. Then ask what he thinks you put inside to make that noise. Encourage him to explain his choice. Work through three of the items in this way. Then ask him to guess what the fourth will sound like, and let him test his prediction.

Taking it further

● Try other things in the tin, encouraging your child to guess whether they will make loud or soft noises, and to lay the items out in a row from quietest to loudest.

LEARNING OPPORTUNITY
● To link two statements, using pictures as a cue to an appropriate follow-up statement.

YOU WILL NEED
Paper; pencil.

Who will fix it?

Sharing the game

● Make four simple drawings of a tooth, an arm in a sling, a car with a flat tyre and a dripping tap.

● Invite your child to play a game with you. Show her the pictures and say that these will help her to play the game.

● Now explain that you will say a sentence, stopping half-way through. Tell your child that, when you stop, you want her to pick up

a picture that has something to do with what you have said. Tell her to say something about the picture that will finish what you said, and make sense.

● Tell your child that you are going to start the first sentence, saying, 'I had to go to the hospital last week, because...'. Encourage her to pick up the picture of the arm in a sling and to add something to your sentence, such as, 'I had fallen over and hurt my arm'.

● Use similar statements to introduce the remaining pictures:
'I had to take the car to the garage last week, because...'
'I had to go to the dentist last week, because...'
'I had to telephone the plumber last week, because...'.

Taking it further

● Make up further starter sentences for your child to complete without picture cues.

● Say a sentence, asking your child to change something in one half of the sentence so that it makes sense, for example, 'The dog growled because someone it knew well came to the door' or 'I don't need to take my umbrella today because it is going to rain'.

 STEPPING STONE
Link statements and stick to a main theme.

EARLY LEARNING GOAL
Communication, language and literacy: Speak clearly and audibly with confidence.

LEARNING
OPPORTUNITY
● To use a picture and a
simple idea as the
starting-point for a story.

YOU WILL NEED
Paper; pencil.

Tools for the job

Sharing the game
● Make four simple drawings of a needle and thread, a hammer and nails, a tube of glue and a spanner.
● Show your child the pictures, explaining that he is going to use them to tell some stories.
● Say that you will give him a clue to the first story. Ask him to look at the pictures and choose what he would use to mend a broken chair.
● When your child has chosen the hammer and nails, say, 'That's what the Daddy Bear in the story chose to mend Baby Bear's chair. A little girl with blond hair sat on it and broke it. Can you guess what the story is?'.
● Ask him to tell you the story of 'Goldilocks and the Three Bears' (Traditional) and how Daddy Bear mended the chair with the hammer and nails.
● Next, ask what he would use to mend a hole in a pocket. Ask if he can make up a story about a little boy who lost something important through the hole. Help him by asking appropriate questions about the main character and the events of the story.
● Use the same idea to begin stories about a car that broke down on an important journey, and a very precious toy that got broken when two children were having an argument.

Taking it further
● Use everyday objects to cue your child into telling well-known stories, such as a plaster, which 'reminds me of a story of two children who came tumbling down a hill'.

STEPPING STONE
Begin to be aware
of the way stories are
structured.

EARLY LEARNING
GOAL
Communication,
language and literacy:
Explore and experiment
with sounds, words and
texts.

LEARNING OPPORTUNITY
● To be able to select one word from a group of three that does not rhyme with the other two.

YOU WILL NEED
A copy of the sets of words (see right).

 STEPPING STONE Understand the concept of a word.

 EARLY LEARNING GOAL Communication, language and literacy: Explore and experiment with sounds, words and texts.

Find the stranger

Sharing the game

● Explain to your child that you are going to play a word game together. Tell her that you are going to say three words, one after the other. Say that you want her to listen carefully and to tell you which of the three words does not rhyme with the other two.

● Before you begin the game, say, 'Let's just try a few words first to see if you can hear whether they rhyme or not. Do dog and log rhyme?'. Wait for her answer and then ask if 'hat' and 'pig' rhyme. Remind her that rhyming words have the same sound at the end.

● Now work through each of these sets of words. Before each set, say, 'Here are the three words. Listen carefully. Which word does not rhyme with the other two?'. Say the words with a slight pause between each one. Try to say them in an even tone so that your expression does not give away the odd one out.

hat	mat	cup
dog	mug	frog
men	ten	tip
sun	log	run
peg	leg	hug
bun	wet	net

Taking it further

● Write all of the words from the sets above on to pieces of card. Help your child to look at the endings of the words and to group them in rhyming sets. See how many of the words do not belong in any rhyming group.

PUZZLE IT OUT

Letter box

LEARNING OPPORTUNITY
● To match sounds with appropriate letters that represent them.

YOU WILL NEED
A cardboard box; six envelopes glue; scissors; 18 pieces of thin card 7cm x 5cm; pencil; marker pen.

Sharing the game

● Write each of the words below, in lower case, on a piece of card. Draw simple pictures on the back of the cards, to illustrate each word.

cat	dog	bag	sun	pen	hat
cup	duck	bat	sock	peg	hill
can	doll	bin	sad	pan	hut

● Glue the envelopes around the sides of the box, to form pockets. On each pocket write the initial letter for one of the sets of words. Use lower-case letters.

● Shuffle the cards and place them, picture up, on the table. Invite your child to play a game.

● Tell your child to pick up the first picture and say what he can see. Ask which sound he hears at the beginning of the word. Say that you would like him to put the card into the pocket on the box with the letter that 'writes' the sound he has said. If necessary, help him by showing him the word on the back of the card and encouraging him to match the first letter to the correct letter on one of the pockets.

● Continue in this way until all the picture cards have been correctly 'pocketed'.

Taking it further

● Add further pockets, with different initial letters to the box. Make more cards with matching initial sounds, making sure that you choose simple words for the cards.

 STEPPING STONE Hear and say the initial sound in words and know which letters represent some of the sounds.

⭐ **EARLY LEARNING GOAL**
Communication, language and literacy: Hear and say initial sound in words.

LEARNING OPPORTUNITY
● To begin to read a number of simple, familiar words.

YOU WILL NEED
A set of cards as described in the game 'Letter box' on page 109; a further 18 pieces of card; marker pen.

 STEPPING STONE Begin to recognise some familiar words.

 EARLY LEARNING GOAL Communication, language and literacy: Read a range of familiar and common words.

Same word?

Sharing the game
● Write the same words on the second set of cards as are written on the first. Use lower-case letters, trying to match the appearance of each word as closely as possible in size and formation to its matching pair. Do not add pictures on the back. Lay both sets of cards out on different sides of the table. All the cards should be word-side up.

● Explain to your child that you are going to play a matching game. Invite her to pick up one of the cards from the set with the pictures on the back.
● Now encourage her to try to read the word on her chosen card. Help her to sound out the initial letter, or all the letters, as appropriate for her current stage of development. Tell her to turn the card over to look at the picture and check what the word says.
● When your child is sure of the word, ask her to look very carefully at the other set of cards and to try to find one with the same word written on it. When she finds the card, remind her of what the first card said and ask what the word on the second card must say as well.
● Repeat the procedure, until all the cards have been paired.

Taking it further
● Lay out all the cards, word-side up, on the table. Ask your child if she can find two cards which both, for example, have the word 'dog' written on them.

CHAPTER 8

JUST YOU AND ME

Young children acquire language skills through a process of listening, trial and error, and modification. As they listen to others speaking, patterns in language begin to emerge. Children then practise their observations in their own language. The more language they hear, the more they can refine their observations and improve their skills. There is no better 'teacher' of language skills for a child than an interested adult who can provide a good model of a wide range of language. Most important of all is that the adult shows real interest in talking with and listening to the child.

DEVELOPING LISTENING SKILLS

In order to develop good language skills, young children need to be able to sustain attentive listening. This is crucial for all aspects of language development, whether it be the learning of new vocabulary or picking up on the individual sounds that go to make up words. The child who can listen carefully will quickly notice that a new word has occurred in conversation. She will listen to the words around it to try to make sense of it, or will listen carefully to your explanation of its meaning, and store it away for future use. The child who is attentive to the sounds around her will hear similarities and differences between speech sounds in words and will be at an advantage when it comes to learning the link between those sounds and the letter or letters that represent them.

How you can help

● Provide a good model by listening carefully when your child talks to you. Treat her questions seriously, and try to find out the answers if you do not already know them.

● Play a game in which you sit absolutely quietly for a minute and listen to every single sound you can hear, from the creaking of a window, to a passing car, or footsteps in the street outside. Try the game in different locations, and talk, at the end of the minute, about the sounds that you have both heard.

● Record some everyday noises, such as a tap running or a door slamming, then play the tape to your child and ask her to guess what the sounds are. You could also play commercially made 'Sound lotto' games.

● Turn the television sound down to show your child how much we can learn about what is going on in a programme by listening carefully as well as by watching it.

LEARNING GOOD LANGUAGE SKILLS

Having a good role model is an enormous asset in the acquisition of language skills. The adult who spends time talking to a child provides an ongoing example of the ways in which we use language. The broader the range of words used by that adult, the broader the child's experience of language will be. The child who hears a variety of sentence structures, such as statements, questions, commands and exclamations, will develop an understanding of how we put language together to convey meaning. If he can, in addition, witness a variety of social interchanges, he will become familiar with the conventions of our language, and be confident in using it to communicate.

How you can help
● Do not talk down to your child by automatically simplifying language. Rather, be prepared to explain to him anything that he does not understand.
● Enrich your child's experience of language by using a broad range of vocabulary when talking to him. Help him to understand, for example, that there are many words other than 'nice' that can be used to describe a pleasurable experience.
● Involve your child in conversations with other adults, whenever it is appropriate.
● Talk with your child about his daily experiences, giving him as much opportunity as possible to put his language skills into practice. Ask him questions that stimulate him to describe people and places and to verbalise feelings and ideas.

LEARNING TO ENJOY LANGUAGE
In providing your child with pleasurable opportunities to rehearse language skills, you will encourage her to want to explore the possibilities of language in all its forms, spoken and written. The key is to have fun together.

How you can help
● Create special times with your child when you sit and talk with her, making sure that you listen to her, giving her your undivided attention.
● Enjoy being silly with language sometimes. See who can make up the silliest statement, such as, 'I saw a pig in the park, roller-skating down the slide'.
● Think of onomatopoeic words (ones that sound like their meaning), such as 'slurp' and 'squelch'. Talk about them with your child, and make up your own.
● Read nonsense verse to your child.

LEARNING TO ENJOY BOOKS
It is never too early to provide young children with the experience of books. Children who are given the opportunity to enjoy pictures and stories at an early age will already be acquiring some of the skills that they will need later, as they embark on the road to reading. Sharing books with an adult gives a young child the opportunity to develop a range of language skills that will benefit him in every area of his education.

How you can help
● Develop a love of stories in your child by telling your own special family stories, based on photograph albums or family events. Encourage your child, as well, to make up stories with you.
● Make sure that your child sees you reading and enjoying the activity.
● Read regularly to your child. Make it a special time when you give him your undivided attention. Read with expression. Pause at exciting points in stories to allow time for your child to say what he thinks might happen next. Talk to him about the pictures as well as the characters.
● Help your child to get to know your local library, so that a wider range of books will be available to him. Invite him to choose books regularly and talk with him about his choices.
● Encourage your child's use of non-fiction as well as fiction. Pursue his interests by helping him to find books on subjects that he wants to explore.
● Let your child hold books and turn the pages as you read to him.
● Bring books to life by, for example, making porridge after reading the traditional story 'Goldilocks and the Three Bears'.

LEARNING OPPORTUNITY
● To become confident in taking part in, and to enjoy, one-to-one conversation.

YOU WILL NEED
Paper; colouring materials.

 STEPPING STONE
Listen to others in one-to-one groups when conversation interests them.

 EARLY LEARNING GOAL
Communication, language and literacy: Enjoy listening to and using spoken language.

You're special

Sharing the game

● Call your child to sit with you, and explain that you are going to play a game in which you each have to tell the other person what is very special about them.

● Say that you will begin the game so that he will know exactly what to do. Begin your sentence with the statement, 'You're special because…' adding something positive about your child. It could be something like, '… you make me smile'.

● Now ask your child to tell you something that is special about you. Encourage him to begin the sentence in the same way as you did.

● Continue to take it in turns in this way. Try to make your comments personal to your child. You might say, for example, 'You build brilliant LEGO models' or 'You paint wonderful pictures'. Above all, try to make statements about who your child is as a person, and not about behaviour. Make your enjoyment of your individual child come through in what you say. Every child will gain confidence from being told things such as, 'You give the best cuddles in the whole wide world'.

Taking it further

● Celebrate each other's specialness by making a 'You're special' card for each other.

● On a large sheet of paper draw and colour a tree trunk, with bare branches. Make this a 'growing tree' of your child's achievements. Add a paper leaf for each new milestone, whether it be tying shoelaces or swimming without armbands. Write the achievement on the leaf, and glue it on to the tree together.

LEARNING OPPORTUNITY
● To respond to nursery rhymes by asking and talking about why certain things may have happened.

YOU WILL NEED
Any book of nursery rhymes.

 STEPPING STONE
Question why things happen, and give explanations.

 EARLY LEARNING GOAL
Communication, language and literacy: Listen with enjoyment, and respond to rhymes and poems.

Perhaps...

Sharing the game
● Invite your child to come and share the book of nursery rhymes with you.
● Read a rhyme such as 'Humpty Dumpty' (Traditional) together. Say that you have noticed that nursery rhymes often do not tell you the whole story and that this one does not tell you why Humpty was sitting on the wall. Ask your child what she thinks Humpty might have been doing there.
● Choose another rhyme, such as 'Little Bo Peep'

(Traditional), and, after you have read it, point out that you cannot tell from the rhyme how Bo Peep lost her sheep. Ask your child what she thinks happened. Does she think that Bo Peep was not watching her sheep properly, or that the sheep ran away?
● With the next rhyme, ask your child if there is anything that she would like to know that the rhyme does not tell her. Encourage her to suggest possible answers to any questions that she comes up with.

Taking it further
● Whenever you read to your child, encourage her to talk about the book or story afterwards. Invite her to tell you what she particularly enjoyed or did not enjoy. Encourage her to ask questions about anything that she feels the story does not fully explain.
● Try making up stories together about what might happen in the future to characters in stories or rhymes that you read. For example, in 'Little Boy Blue' (Traditional), what does your child think will happen to the boy who should be looking after the sheep? What will the farmer say when he finds out he is asleep?

JUST YOU AND ME

LEARNING OPPORTUNITY
● To build up a story and suggest how it might end.

YOU WILL NEED
Pictures of children, places and animals cut from magazines (or drawings); roll of paper, or pieces of paper taped together; Blu-Tack; torch.

STEPPING STONE
Suggest how the story might end.

EARLY LEARNING GOAL
Communication, language and literacy: Show an understanding of the elements of stories.

Torchlight tales

Sharing the game
● Attach a length of paper along a wall with Blu-Tack. Tape a picture of an animal on to the frieze. Add a picture of a place. Choose one that would be a strange place to find your chosen animal, for example, a supermarket to follow a picture of a cow. Add the picture of a person. Draw an empty square at the end.
● Pull the curtains and switch off the light to darken the room. Invite your child to join you for a story.
● Shine the torch on the animal and introduce it. Describe a character who wanders off from home to explore, or a cow who is tired of eating grass and decides to look for something new to eat, which is how she ends up in a…
● Light up the second picture and describe the chaos that the animal causes there. Just as the chaos reaches its height, explain that rescue arrives in the shape of…
● Light up the third picture and introduce the owner of the animal. Say, 'And what do you think (s)he did?'. Move to the blank square and let your child finish the story.

Taking it further
● Encourage your child to draw a picture to go in the blank square.
● Make your child the hero of the story by naming the cow's owner after him.
● Help your child to choose pictures or draw them, to make up his own torchlight tale.

JUST YOU AND ME

LEARNING OPPORTUNITY
● To tell a story, remembering the correct sequence of events, and adding to it.

YOU WILL NEED
Just you and your child.

 STEPPING STONE
Listen to and join in with stories, one-to-one.

 EARLY LEARNING GOAL
Communication, language and literacy: Retell narratives in the correct sequence, drawing on language patterns of stories.

My friend Freddie

Sharing the game
● Ask your child to help you to make up a story. Explain that it is a story about a friend of yours called Freddie, who went shopping and had a huge long list of things to buy. Say that you will start the story, but that you would like your child to fill in some parts of it.

● Start by saying, 'My friend Freddie went to the shops to buy a bunch of bananas and …'. Ask your child to add something that she thinks Freddie might have bought there as well.

● Repeat the story line, including your child's suggestion, and add something else to the list. Then ask your child to repeat the whole list and add something else.

● When you have about six items in the list, say, 'Oh, I forgot to tell you why Freddie needed the bananas. I'd better start again. My friend Freddie went to the shops to buy a bunch of bananas for his pet gorilla'. Now ask your child why Freddie needed the first thing your child suggested. Build up the story again, making the reasons as funny as you can. Finish it off with Freddie staggering home with a heavy shopping basket.

Taking it further
● Build new elements into the storytelling when you play the game on different occasions. Try adding what happens each time Freddie gets home with an item, saying, for example, 'When he gave the bananas to his gorilla…' and adding something amusing. Or you could have Freddie eat the bananas before he gets home, lose other things and give some things away.

LEARNING OPPORTUNITY
● To ask simple questions and to use descriptive words.

YOU WILL NEED
Pictures of animals stuck on to pieces of card.

STEPPING STONE
Ask simple questions.

EARLY LEARNING GOAL
Communication, language and literacy: Interact with others, taking turns in conversation.

Tell me some more

Sharing the game
● Spread the pictures out on a table, face-down. Ask your child to choose a card, and to tell you what is in the picture.
● When your child has told you, for example, that it is a lion, say, 'Tell me some more. Is it a fierce lion?'. After your child has answered, repeat the information back to him in the form of a statement, such as, 'It is a picture of a fierce lion'.

● Add another question, 'Tell me some more. Does it have a shaggy mane?'. When you have the answer, include this information in a statement, for example, 'It is a picture of a fierce lion, with a shaggy mane'. Continue in this way, until you run out of questions, and have a detailed description of the animal.
● Now choose a card yourself, and tell your child to ask you questions about it. Encourage him to repeat back the information you give him each time, by saying, for example, 'So, what sort of an animal is in my picture?'. Help him to remember as much of what you have said as possible.

Taking it further
● Use a different set of pictures, for example, of vehicles or places (use pictures cut from magazines), to encourage your child to ask a different set of questions and to use different descriptive vocabulary.
● Respond positively to questions your child asks on a daily basis. Remark on what a good question it is. If you do not know the answer, say that you will try to find out together. Share in his curiosity by saying that you have always wondered about that, too.

Rhyming riddles

Sharing the game
● Invite your child to play a rhyming game with you.
● Explain that you are going to say a rhyme to your child. Say that it is a sort of riddle. Tell her that you will miss out the last word of the rhyme and that you want her to guess what that word should be.
● Explain that your child should listen carefully, because there will be two clues to the word in what you say. Tell her that one clue will be in the first line of the rhyme. This clue will tell her something about the word she is looking for. The next clue will come in the second line of the rhyme, and this will tell her a part of her body that rhymes with the missing word. Say that both these clues will help her to think of the missing word.

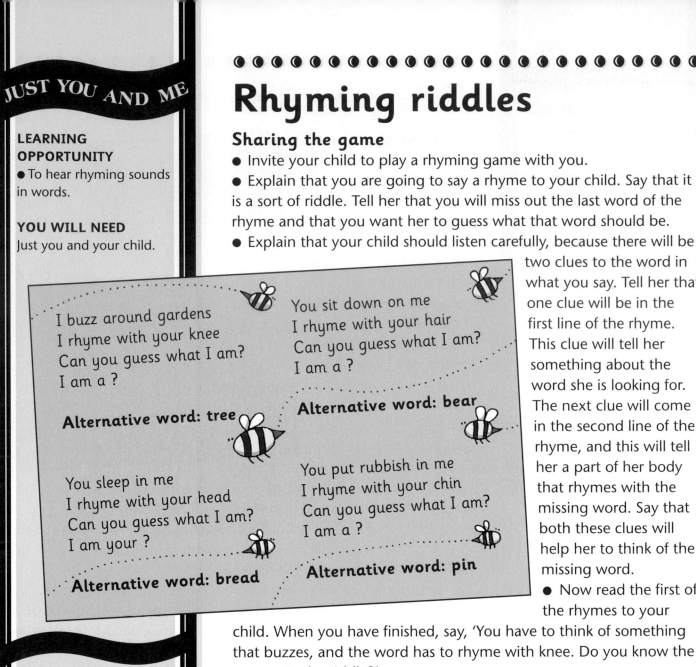

I buzz around gardens
I rhyme with your knee
Can you guess what I am?
I am a ?

Alternative word: tree

You sit down on me
I rhyme with your hair
Can you guess what I am?
I am a ?

Alternative word: bear

You sleep in me
I rhyme with your head
Can you guess what I am?
I am your ?

Alternative word: bread

You put rubbish in me
I rhyme with your chin
Can you guess what I am?
I am a ?

Alternative word: pin

● Now read the first of the rhymes to your child. When you have finished, say, 'You have to think of something that buzzes, and the word has to rhyme with knee. Do you know the answer to the riddle?'.
● If your child is having difficulty, supply two possible answers, such as 'fly' and 'bee', asking which rhymes with knee.

Taking it further
● You will find, underneath each riddle on this page, an alternative rhyming word. Talk about these rhyming words with your child and encourage her to help you make up first-line clues for them to be used in riddles. Help her to try out the riddles that she makes on another family member, or friend.

STEPPING STONE
Show awareness of rhyme.

EARLY LEARNING GOAL
Communication, language and literacy:
Hear and say final sounds in words.

LEARNING OPPORTUNITY
● To listen carefully to stories and be able to retell them in the proper order.

YOU WILL NEED
A shoelace; coloured beads.

STEPPING STONE
Listen to stories with increasing attention and recall.

EARLY LEARNING GOAL
Communication, language and literacy: Enjoy listening to and using spoken language.

Story beads

Sharing the game
● Think up a very simple story to tell your child. The story should involve a series of colours. You might, for example, tell the story of a small child getting dressed for a party, mentioning each item of clothing the child puts on, and its colour.
● Explain to your child that you are going to tell a story and that, afterwards, you want him to tell

the story back to you. Say that you will show him how to use the beads to help him remember what happens in the story.
● Tell the story. Each time you mention a colour, thread a bead of a matching colour on to the shoelace. Say something like, 'Remember, she put on her blue vest first'.
● Ask your child to tell you the story, using the beads to remind him of the order of the clothes the child put on. Tell him to take a matching bead off the shoelace each time he mentions a colour.

Taking it further
● Link two items to each bead in the telling of the story, for example, blue socks as well as a blue vest.
● Make the story more complex by adding in extra events between the mention of each colour. See if your child can remember these as well as the items linked to the coloured beads.

LEARNING OPPORTUNITY
● To retell the story of her life so far.

YOU WILL NEED
A long length of string; pegs; photographs of your child.

STEPPING STONE
Begin to be aware of the way stories are structured.

EARLY LEARNING GOAL
Communication, language and literacy: Retell narratives in the correct sequence, drawing on language patterns of stories.

This is my life

Sharing the game
● Tie the string to two chairs, stretching it across the room like a line. Arrange all the photographs in chronological order and have the pegs ready.

● Invite your child to come and hear a very special story about a very special person.
● Pick up the first photograph and peg it to the left end of the line. Use a story format to tell your child about the photograph. Say, for example, 'Once upon a time there lived a little baby girl called… She was born on…'.
● Peg up the next photograph and weave this into the story. As you move from one photo to another, use the sort of phrase that you might hear in a story-book, such as, 'A year passed before…' and 'Just as her parents had promised…'.
● Do not let your child see which photo is coming next. Pause occasionally, and ask her what she thinks might happen next, just as you might if you were reading her a story.
● When you have finished, tell your child that you would really enjoy it if she would tell you the story. Suggest that she call her story 'This is my life' and encourage her to go back to the first photograph and to begin her storytelling.

Taking it further
● Hunt out some photographs of yourself and tell your life story. Sit and talk with your child about how the stories are different.
● Use family photograph albums as the basis for storytelling sessions.

LEARNING OPPORTUNITY
● To understand that marks can have a meaning.

YOU WILL NEED
A calendar with room to write in the daily sections; pencil.

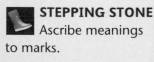
STEPPING STONE
Ascribe meanings to marks.

EARLY LEARNING GOAL
Communication, language and literacy: Attempt writing for different purposes, such as stories.

Do you remember?

Sharing the game
● As preparation, keep a note of the things that your child does each day, over the course of a week. Jot down one thing each day, even something as simple as watching a favourite television programme.

● Invite your child to help you make a note of everything he has done over the week. Show him how the calendar has a section for each day.

● Talk through his week, a day at a time. Help him to remember what he did on each day, giving him clues if necessary. Suggest that he draw something in the section of the calendar for that day, to remind him of what he did. For example, a drawing of a book could stand for a library visit, some waves could be the symbol for a trip to the swimming baths, a television could represent viewing a favourite programme, and so on. If your child finds this difficult, help him by drawing things for him.

● When you have filled in a symbol for each day of the week, look back at them, saying, 'What a busy week you had. Let's see, on Monday you…'. Encourage your child to look at the calendar and tell you what he did each day.

Taking it further
● Help your child to mark on the calendar some of the things that he will be doing over the next couple of weeks, using similar symbols.
● Use the record on the calendar as the basis of a letter to a family member, such as a grandparent. Encourage your child to write about his week, using the pictures from the calendar, with you adding explanatory words.

LEARNING OPPORTUNITY
● To use books to find out information.

YOU WILL NEED
A small selection of children's non-fiction books on subjects that interest your child.

 STEPPING STONE
Know that information can be retrieved from books and computers.

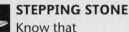 **EARLY LEARNING GOAL**
Communication, language and literacy: Show an understanding of how information can be found in non-fiction texts to answer questions about where, who, why and how.

Under my arm

Sharing the game
● Look through one of the books, making a mental note of a few facts. If your child likes wild animals, for example, you might look up something on the subject of elephants.
● Sit down with the book tucked under your arm. Tell your child, 'I've got an elephant under my arm'. When she protests, repeat your statement, adding, 'It's an African elephant. I know that because it's got big ears'. Add another fact or two.
● Ask your child if she would like to see the elephant. Show her an illustration in the book. Point to the text and tell her that you found out about the elephant from there. Ask if she would like to know more. Read more of the book together.
● Change to another subject, tucking a different interesting item under your arm, in the form of an appropriate book. Encourage your child to look through different books, to choose something to put under her own arm, to tell you about.

Taking it further
● Explore further books to find out even more about your child's special interests.
● Go on a 'Let's-find-out safari' to your local library. Choose a subject that your child would like to know more about. Make the trip an adventure by dressing in 'space suits' to find out about space, or taking a pair of 'binoculars' made from kitchen rolls to find out about wildlife, and taking 'space food' or an 'explorer's snack' with you.

LEARNING OPPORTUNITY
● To practise writing simple regular words.

LEARNING OPPORTUNITY
● To practise writing simple regular words.

YOU WILL NEED
Paper; pencils; cards with a picture or drawing on one side and the appropriate word on the other, featuring the following items: cat, dog, rat, frog, duck, hen, bag, tin, pan, net, cup, jug.

STEPPING STONE
Ascribe meanings to marks.

EARLY LEARNING GOAL
Communication, language and literacy: Use their phonic knowledge to write simple regular words.

Guess what!

Sharing the game
● Invite your child to play a guessing game with you. Go through each card, pointing to the word, and drawing attention to the initial letter as you say the word. Turn the card over and show the picture.
● Decide on a card, without saying what it is. Place it on the table, word-side showing, with three or four other cards. Select cards that have something in common with your chosen card. If it is 'cat', for example, lay out the other animal cards as well.
● Now tell your child that you are thinking of one of the words. Give him clues, which gradually narrow down the possibilities. For 'cat', these might be:
  – it is an animal
  – it has a tail
  – it has two ears
  – it has four legs
  – it likes milk.
● Ask your child to guess the word and to copy it down from the card. Help him to write it, if necessary, or accept just the first letter. Now tell him the word that you had in mind and let him turn over the card that he copied to check the picture and see if he was right.
● Play again, choosing a different card. A good starting-point for clues for the non-animal words is 'We can put things in this'.

Taking it further
● Lay out a larger number of cards for your child to choose from.
● Add new cards, with items such as a van, jet, bus, bat, ham, jam, man, doll, cot, box, lid, hat, cap, pen and mug.

LEARNING OPPORTUNITY
● To use writing to communicate a message.

YOU WILL NEED
Paper; pencils; colouring pencils or pens; soft toy with a care label attached (optional).

STEPPING STONE
Use writing as a means of recording and communicating.

EARLY LEARNING GOAL
Communication, language and literacy: Attempt writing for different purposes.

Look after me

Sharing the game

● Suggest to your child that she might like to make a booklet to remind you of what she likes and does not like. Say that it will help you to look after her properly. If you have a soft toy with a care label, explain to her how it helps the owner to know how to look after the toy.

● Fold a few sheets of paper in half to form a booklet. Write 'How to look after…' on the cover, helping your child to add her own name. On the first page, write 'Foods I like', encouraging your child to try to list her favourite foods. Accept initial letters or any attempts at writing. Write the correct form of words beside your child's attempt, if she would like you to.

● Continue, using headings such as, 'Foods I don't like', 'Clothes I like to wear', 'My favourite toys', 'Places I like to go' and so on. If necessary, write for your child, in order for her to complete the book as she would like. Encourage her to illustrate the pages, and display the finished item prominently. Refer to it now and then in choosing clothes or cooking her a favourite meal.

Taking it further

● Help your child to see writing as a means of communication by leaving her notes to find, asking simple things, such as what she would like for tea or whether she has had a good day. Provide plenty of writing materials for her to be able to reply to your notes and to write whenever she wants.

RESOURCES

This page can be used in conjunction with the game on page 63.

Active alphabet

Call out the letter name, the sound, then the word (in bold). Emphasise the appropriate letter sound as you give the word. Give the instruction (in italics) as you demonstrate the action.

a – **attention** – *Stand to attention, really straight, arms by your side.*

b – **bend** – *Bend over slowly, until your fingers touch your toes.*

c – **curl** – *Curl up into a tight ball.*

d – **dance** – *Dance around in a circle.*

e – **exercise** – *Do star jump exercises.*

f – **flop** – *Bend over, let your arms and head hang, make yourself flop.*

g – **gallop** – *Gallop around the room.*

h – **hop** – *Hop on one leg.*

i – **invisible** – *Make yourself as small as you can, try to be invisible.*

j – **jump** – *Jump up and down on the spot.*

k – **kick** – *Kick one leg at a time as high as you can.*

l – **lie down** – *Lie down and rest.*

m – **march** – *March around the room.*

n – **non-stop running** – *Run around without stopping.*

o – **on-the-spot running** – *Run on the spot.*

p – **pause** – *Take a pause, sit down and be peaceful.*

q – **quiet** – *Make sure that you are really quiet.*

r – **roll** – *Roll over and over on the floor.*

s – **skip** – *Stand up and skip around.*

t – **tiptoe** – *Walk on tiptoe.*

u – **upside-down** – *Turn upside-down.*

v – **vanish** – *Make yourself really small again as if you wanted to vanish.*

w – **walk** – *Stand up and just walk around slowly.*

x – **exhausted** – *Are you exhausted now? Look really tired.*

y – **yawn** – *If you're tired, give a big yawn.*

z – **zigzag** – *You're so tired you can't walk straight. You can only zigzag. Lie down and go to sleep – zzzzzzzzzzz.*

Shape up

Use these pictures to help you with the game described on page 76.

Swap it

Make the words listed below by combining your word-ending cards with home-made alphabet cards (see page 81).

 at   mat, bat, cat, sat, fat, hat, pat

 ad   dad, had, mad, sad, pad

 in   bin, din, fin, pin, tin, win

 ip   dip, lip, rip, pip, sip, tip

 en   den, hen, men, pen, ten

 ug   bug, hug, mug, rug, tug, dug

 ot   dot, cot, lot, not, rot, tot, pot

Clowning around

Follow the stages shown here to draw a clown (see page 75).

1 2 3 4 5 6 7 8

Cheese straws

What you need

flour

grated cheese

margarine

water to mix

What to do

1 Rub the margarine into the flour.

2 Add the cheese.

3 Add water.

4 Roll out the dough.

5 Cut into straws.

6 Bake at 200°C (Gas Mark 6) for ten minutes.